Happiness as Actuality in *Nicomachean Ethics*

An Overview

Happiness as Actuality in *Nicomachean Ethics*

An Overview

Sorin Sabou

PICKWICK *Publications* • Eugene, Oregon

HAPPINESS AS ACTUALITY IN NICOMACHEAN ETHICS
An Overview

Pickwick Publications
An Imprint of Wipf and Stock Publishers
199 W. 8th Ave., Suite 3
Eugene, OR 97401

www.wipfandstock.com

PAPERBACK ISBN: 978-1-5326-5990-4
HARDCOVER ISBN: 978-1-5326-5991-1
EBOOK ISBN: 978-1-5326-5992-8

Cataloguing-in-Publication data:

Names: Sabou, Sorin, author.

Title: Happiness as actuality in Nicomachean Ethics : an overview / Sorin Sabou.

Description: Eugene, OR: Pickwick Publications, 2018 | Includes bibliographical references.

Identifiers: ISBN 978-1-5326-5990-4 (paperback) | ISBN 978-1-5326-5991-1 (hardcover) | ISBN 978-1-5326-5992-8 (ebook)

Subjects: LCSH: Aristotle—Nicomachean ethics | Aristotle—Contributions in concept of happiness | Ethics, Ancient | Aristotle | Happiness—History

Classification: B430.A5 NUMBER 2018 (paperback) | B430.A5 (ebook)

Manufactured in the U.S.A.   09/27/18 *for Simona, Andra, and Dora*

CONTENTS

CHAPTER 1

INTRODUCTION

1.1 THE TOPIC

THIS PROJECT IS AN inquiry into the meaning of happiness [εὐδαιμονία] in Aristotle's *Nicomachean Ethics* (*EN*). It seeks to offer a correct interpretation of Aristotle's virtue ethic as found in *EN*. As such, it is not an inquiry in various contemporary developments of Aristotelian virtue ethics, so I will restrict my interlocutors to those scholars who focus on exegeting *EN*.

The conceptual background of my argument is given by the whole work of *EN* and all other works of Aristotle.[1] Every major concept and idea found in *EN* will be interpreted in the context of the text read as a whole and then will be explored within the context of in the entire Aristotelian corpus for acquiring a better understanding of how Aristotle[2] used and integrated that particular concept. Based on this method, then I will argue for a particular interpretation of the concept under investigation. In this way, I will try to allow Aristotle to speak for himself.

It is irrelevant whether I agree with Aristotle or not; what matters, for my argument, is to elucidate what Aristotle says about the matter under

---

1. For the historical background of Aristotle's life in relation to *EN* see Crisp, "Aristotle: Ethics and Politics," 110–13, Pakaluk, *Nicomachean Ethics*, 16–22, Bobonich, "Aristotle's Ethical Treaties," 14–15, Cooper, "Political Community," 212–24, Hughes, *Nicomachean Ethics*, 3–8.

2. For the most recent biography of Aristotle see Natali, *Aristotle*, 5–71.

investigation. It is essential for the interpreter to be as aware as possible of his/her own framework of thought and not try to impose it on the subject of his/her research. For example, I am a Pauline scholar doing research in the Graeco-Roman world of antiquity. So, I am not an Aristotelian philosopher, but I will try as hard as possible to keep my own convictions away, and let Aristotle speak for himself. This book is not a dialogue between my ideas and Aristotle's ideas about happiness.

This point is important because, as I will show later in this project, the vast majority of contemporary scholarly research on Aristotle's ethics is done within a secular perspective, and because of this, it tries hard to eliminate everything in Aristotle that does not fit a secular reading of his writings. This is my major criticism towards my interlocutors: even if they say that their work is about what Aristotle wrote about a particular topic, they offer an interpretation of Aristotle through their own secular lenses, without letting *all* the Aristotelian available data to speak for itself. My point is that every major concept used by Aristotle, like "final end"/τέλος, "function of man"/ἔργον ἀνθρώπου, "contemplation"/θεωρία, "imprint"/ τύπος, "intellect"/νοῦς, etc., has to be interpreted in the larger Aristotelian worldview. Thus, the conceptual background argued for in this book includes everything that we have from Aristotle about various topics relevant for my specific focus, which is the meaning of happiness in *EN*.

The ancient Greek conceptual background on εὐδαιμονία is presented in detail in a separate section: 3.3—From Sappho to Lycurgus: Pre-Aristotelian Literature on εὐδαιμονία.

1.2 THE THESIS

My thesis about the meaning of happiness in *EN* is that Aristotle understands εὐδαιμονία as "actuality." He uses two main metaphors to explain it: 1) the perimeter of the good, and 2) the imprint of happiness. These two metaphors are found in Aristotle's argument in *EN* at two major signposts: I.7 1098a22 and X.9 1179a35.

I will argue that the "perimeter of the good" is a political metaphor used by Aristotle to delineate the perimeter of his inquiry. This delineation is achieved with the help of two distinct criteria: the criterion of finality and the criterion of the function. Aristotle understands happiness as the ultimate aim [τέλος] and as the function of man [ἔργον ἀνθρώπου]. These criteria are metaphysical concepts that integrate Aristotle's ethical inquiry as a political, metaphysical, and teleological enterprise.

Then, I will argue that the "imprint of happiness" is an educational metaphor, which, in the delineated perimeter of the good, forms the best form of life, a life in which the virtuous intellect inquires and contemplates [θεωρία]. This "type of happiness" is the final end of the most authoritative science, the science of politics. Thus, for Aristotle εὐδαιμονία in *EN* is τέλος and ἔργον ἀνθρώπου as these reach completions in θεωρία.

Εὐδαιμονία as the ultimate aim of man, in *EN*, is understood correctly only if the larger metaphysical framework of Aristotle is in the background. Εὐδαιμονία in *EN*, as the main element of Aristotle's ethics, positions the whole inquiry as a project in teleological metaphysical political ethics.

1.3 THE STRUCTURE OF THE ARGUMENT

I will defend the above thesis by an argument that has the following structure. In Chapter 2, I will present an overview of Aristotle's understanding of εὐδαιμονία in *EN* to explain the details of Aristotle project and also to identify the points of contention in explaining the meaning of εὐδαιμονία. Then, I will present and examine the state of research on εὐδαιμονία. This research focuses on three important questions: 1) what kind of good is happiness? 2) what is the relationship between happiness (*EN*, Books I and II) and complete happiness (*EN*, Book X)? and 3) what is the relationship between happiness and the external goods? The purpose of this second chapter is to present the advance of research done on happiness in *EN* and to show that there are other significant lines of inquiry that are not yet examined.

Then, in Chapter 3, I will present a case for a new reading of Aristotle's entire inquiry on happiness in *EN*. This new reading is based on the importance of two significant signposts (one in *EN* I.7 1098a22, and the other in X.9 1179a35) used by Aristotle to explain his research into the meaning of εὐδαιμονία in *EN*. I will present the evidence for a different translation of the Greek phrases that are usually translated as the "outline of the good" (*EN* I.7 1098a22) and the "outline of happiness" (*EN* X.9 1179a35), which I maintain are better translated as the "perimeter of the good" and as the "imprint of happiness." These different translations signal something of significance that has to be investigated, and that is done in the following two chapters (4 and 5).

3

In Chapter 4, I will explore the "perimeter of the good" by studying the distinct criteria of finality and function. Both these two distinct criteria are, in Aristotle's worldview, metaphysical concepts. The criterion of finality°[τέλος] establishes the overall movement and aim of his inquiry on εὐδαιμονία. Εὐδαιμονία as the "final end" is the self-sufficient aim of all human actions. Aristotle understands it in political terms: this final self-sufficient end is the aim of politics. Aristotle's metaphysical political teleology is the foundation of his teleological ethics. Εὐδαιμονία is a relational political concept; it has to be understood in the light of metaphysics and politics.

The criterion of function [ἔργον ἀνθρώπου] establishes what is the best for man. I will study the "function of man" by focusing on exploring what the "function" is in Aristotle's worldview, then by studying the "activity of the soul," and virtue. I will argue that the "function of man" is a metaphysical teleological concept and constitutes εὐδαιμονία, the good of man. The good of man is an activity of the soul; for man to function well he needs his soul to follow a rational principle. Our aims have to be guided by the dominant role of the rational principle within the soul. Our intellect aims us towards what is most noble and most good. In *EN*, this is εὐδαιμονία, the ultimate and highest good of man. This "activity of the soul" is understood by Aristotle as being "according to virtue." Aristotle understands virtue as a disposition that renders a man as being good and makes him fulfill his function well. This is how the good is the function.

In Chapter 5, I will study the completion of the function argument. The second major interpretative metaphor of the "imprint of happiness" is a complex educational metaphor with multiple features. I will argue that Aristotle's argument from Book X is a continuation of his argument from Books I and II. And what he says in Book X.6–9 is in accord with what he said in the first two books. I will argue that εὐδαιμονία as θεωρία is the teleological metaphysical climax of the whole inquiry in Aristotelian political science. In Aristotle's worldview humans have a composite nature that is oriented teleologically towards its actualization. The perimeter of teleology expands constantly until it reaches actualization, which is "complete happiness." In this perimeter every human person acts according to his/her function. The soul and especially the intellect has to act and be excellent. This is how the virtues are formed. The intellect, the divine element within us, is an element of the human soul and its activity is the activity of θεωρία, which is both study and contemplation. Thus, the connection between divine and human is organic in human life; the intellect cannot be extracted from the soul. It is the ultimate human potentiality for being able to achieve actuality.

In Book X, Aristotle also finalizes his analysis of the role of the external goods. His main point is that man's nature is not self-sufficient for the activity of contemplation. It needs external goods. I argue that the external goods are part of Aristotle's inquiry about εὐδαιμονία because human nature is not self-sufficient. The "need" for external goods has to be understood in instrumental terms. Resources are needed to express and practice εὐδαιμονία. It is not that εὐδαιμονία is accomplished by the external goods but, it is performed with their help. The practice of noble acts with the help of some external goods leads to the development of certain traits of character, but character and virtue are not formed by external goods.

Εὐδαιμονία needs time to establish itself in human life through habituation, and in this way it becomes stable and strong. Usually a future calamity cannot dislodge it (only the very severe and long adversity can do that, and even then, there is a way back to happiness, given enough time).

Chapter 6, the conclusion will bring together my research by focusing on my thesis that in *EN*, for Aristotle, happiness as actuality is to be understood through the lenses of the two major metaphors of the "perimeter of the good" and the "imprint of happiness."

CHAPTER 2

ARISTOTLE'S ETHICAL INQUIRY AND THE SCHOLARLY DEBATES

2.1 INTRODUCTION

IN THIS CHAPTER, I first present Aristotle's line of the inquiry about happiness/εὐδαιμονία in *EN*. My discussion is organized to reflect Aristotle's own sections: an introduction to the good, the finality of happiness, the function of man, human goodness, and contemplation. After that, I will examine the three main questions debated by recent scholars in relation to it: 1) What kind of good is happiness in *EN*? 2) What is the relationship between happiness and complete happiness? and 3) What is the relationship between happiness and the external goods?

This chapter explores the details of what Aristotle considered to be important in identifying the ultimate end of man, and how recent scholars have examined it. Their studies help me to identify significant areas in which work can be done for a different and improved understanding of happiness in *EN*.

2.2 ARISTOTLE'S ETHICAL INQUIRY

In this section, I will present the overall line of inquiry about happiness in *EN*[1]. I will highlight the main moves and topics addressed by Aristotle, and how the reader needs to understand them in the *EN*. I will argue that 1) Aristotle begins with an introduction to his subject by presenting it as a "type/imprint" which is achieved teleologically and politically. Then, 2) he will inquire about the nature of happiness and will say that happiness is the ultimate good, the good in itself, the self-sufficient good. Next, 3) Aristotle will search for a more precise explanation of happiness by studying the function of man. To this, 4) he will add an inquiry into the human goodness, and then, 5) he will complete his study of the function of man by inquiring about the highest virtue, which is the virtue of the highest part of us, the intellect. This overall structure of Aristotle's entire study in *EN* about εὐδαιμονία is presented in a summary below. This summary is organized in these five sections.

2.2.1 An introduction to the good

The main subject of Aristotle's ethical inquiry in *EN* is happiness, the ultimate end of humans. Right from the start, Aristotle positions his inquiry within a teleological perspective. He observes that whatever a human does, that activity has an end in view (*EN* I.1 1094a1). He says that this end or aim is some good. This teleological perspective orders the entire inquiry that follows. The entire search is a search for the ultimate end or the supreme good (*EN* I.2 1094a20).

This search is a scientific search because the supreme good is the object of every science,[2] especially of the science of politics, which, according to Aristotle, is the ruling science, the science with most authority (*EN* I.2 1094a25). This affirmation makes Aristotle's inquiry a political study. This is so, because the science of politics is the science that constitutes the apex of all scientific study, and according to Aristotle, the aim of this science is an aim he claims, that includes the ends of all sciences (*EN* I.2 1094b5). Aristotle understands the science of politics in *EN*, as the "most authoritative

---

1. For the most recent study about the structure of entire *EN*, see Hughes, *Nicomachean Ethics*, 8–18.

2. Aristotle understands the term "science" as "the most rigorous sort of discursive knowledge." (Groarke, *Aristotle: Logic*)

of the sciences" (*EN* I.2 1094b28). This means that the science of politics orders what sciences and what faculties (strategy, economy, oratory, etc.) are needed in the city (*EN* I.2 1094b1). The aims of all of them are included in the aim of the science of politics.

This supreme good is ultimately the good of the state. When Aristotle discusses the good of the individual and the good of the state, he says that the good of the state is greater and more perfect (*EN* I.2 1094b10). This greatness is due to the fact that is harder to achieve and preserve. When it is achieved, this is seen as a noble and divine achievement. "Divinity" here does not point in the direction of religion, but in the direction of metaphysics. To resemble to gods, for Aristotle, means to get closer to your actuality. Actuality is understood as the fulfillment of potentiality. As I will show later in 4.1.2, in Aristotle's worldview, god, the unmoved mover, is the pure actuality towards which everything aims to reach their actuality. Humans in their lives together achieve something of their actuality by securing the good of the state.

But such an ethical inquiry is by no means precise. It is uncertain (*EN* I.3 1094b20). The object of study makes it to be like that; to study the good points the enquirer in various directions. Sometimes good things do not lead to good outcomes. There are situations in which a good thing has bad consequences. For example, a rich person can be ruined by her wealth, or someone who is courageous may lose his life when he acts with courage (*EN* I.3 1094b20). Even when premises are uncertain, and we have to be content with a broad conclusion that depicts a "type" of truth [τύπῳ τἀληθὲς] (*EN* I.3 1094b20), the conclusions are right. I will explain in 3.1.2, how I understand the "type" language in Aristotle's inquiry in *EN*.

When the end of the science of politics is studied, the person who investigates it must be a well-educated person. Such a person also needs the experience of life. Because of this, a young person is not fit to be a student of politics. His/her experience of life, according to Aristotle, is incipient and the feelings are in control of his/her life (*EN* I.3 1095a5). To study politics is not about acquiring knowledge but understanding the action to be accomplished.

At this point in Aristotle's inquiry there is a signpost that identifies everything before it as an "introduction"[3] to the subject of his study (*EN* I.3

---

3. Other scholars translate with "preliminary points" (Irwin, *Nicomachean Ethics*), or "preamble" (Crisp, *Nicomachean Ethics*), "prelude" (Bartlett and Collins, *Nicomachean Ethics*), or "an account" (Reeve, *Nicomachean Ethics*).

1095a12[4]). This introduction to the subject of Aristotle's ethics is composed as a ring composition: it starts with a reference to a "type" of the good (*EN* I.2 1094a25), and it is closed with a reference to a "type" of truth (*EN* I.3 1094b20). Thus, Aristotle's introduction to his ethics has to be seen through the lens of a "type" [τύπος]. Right from the start Aristotle is determined to find what constitutes this "type"[5] of good and, make it a target to aim at. Both the practical and the theoretical sciences aim at it. This inquiry is about achieving an "imprint" of truth. This observation is essential and significant because Aristotle's whole inquiry on happiness in *EN*, when read in the light of X.9 1179b1, is an investigation about a "type" of happiness. I am not aware of any study about εὐδαιμονία in *EN* that mentions and explores this major observation that the overall hermeneutical key to understand εὐδαιμονία in *EN* is τύπος, which means "blow," "the effect of a blow."[6] I will give the details of this understanding of *EN* ins 3.2.2 and 5.2.1.

2.2.2 The finality of happiness

Aristotle resumes his inquiry by discussing about the highest good that can be achieved through action (*EN* I.4 1095a15). From the way he chooses to speak about the good as the highest good it can be seen that his political teleological ethics is oriented upward, towards the "highest" good. He says that there is no debate concerning the name of this highest good; everyone speaks about it as happiness [εὐδαιμονία] (*EN* I.4 1095a20). The disputed thing about the highest good, happiness, is what constitutes it.

Aristotle's argument in identifying what is happiness starts with an inquiry about the good. He observes that there are many good things and beyond them there is a good that is "good in itself" and this good is the "cause" of all other things as being good (*EN* I.4 1095a30). The fact that a thing is good in itself is something proper to it and this feature cannot be taken away easily (*EN* I.5 1095b29).

This insight is based on a metaphysical principle that says: the "first principle is the fact that a thing is so" (*EN* I.4 1095b5). This is explained by Aristotle in terms of a student who studies politics and needs to be very

---

4. Rackham, *Nicomachean Ethics*.

5. The usual translation of τύπος here is "outline" (Rackham, *Nicomachean Ethics*; Irwin, *Nicomachean Ethics*; Reeve, *Nicomachean Ethics*) but, as I will argue in 3.2.2, the better translation is "imprint."

6. Liddell, Scott, Jones, and Mckenzie, *A Greek-English Lexicon*, 1835.

well trained in his habits. Because of this training a good student of politics knows already the first principles. This insight brings forward the long discourse about the virtues accomplished by habituation that will follow beginning with the end of Book II in *EN*.

Some good things are called so by way of proportion (*EN* I.6 1096b30). For example, a comparison: as sight is good in the human body, so the intelligence is good in the human soul (*EN* I.6 1096b30). Something is called good because contributes to the good of other things, sight to the body, intelligence to the soul. Aristotle's point is focused on what later, in Book X, will be explained as the "best part" of us and he will study the virtue of this part. He studies the happiness of humans and this insight about the good by way of proportion gives the reader the element that will come under scrutiny at the end of inquiry, the human intellect.

Then, Aristotle continues his teleological practicable inquiry and explains that the good is the aim and reason of all our activities. We do everything for its sake (*EN* I.7 1097a15), there is nothing beyond it, it is final (*EN* I.7 1097a30). For example, the acquiring of wealth is not a good in itself, we are doing it because through wealth we can do or have other goods. But the supreme good is a good pursued as an end in itself, it is final, it is never a means towards some other good. Aristotle says that this is what type of good happiness is. It is a good we always choose for its own sake and never as a means to something else (*EN* I.7 1097b1).

The same is true in relation to the "self-sufficiency of happiness." Aristotle speaks about "self-sufficiency" as being linked to oneself, and also to others. By nature, every human is a social being (*EN* I.7 1097b15) who lives with others. But something is self-sufficient when it stands by itself having life desirable and lacking in nothing (*EN* I.7 1097b15). Because of its finality and self-sufficiency, Aristotle says, happiness is the end towards which all actions aim (*EN* I.7 1097b20). Thus, the criterion of finality to understand εὐδαιμονία is about being the ultimate end, being the good of the state, an end in itself not a means towards something else, it is about being self-sufficient.

2.2.3 Function of man

Aristotle continues his ethical inquiry because he needs a more explicit understanding of what constitute happiness (*EN* I.7 1097b25). He will be able to be more explicit in explaining happiness by finding out what man's function is (*EN* I.7 1097b25). The criterion of the "function" builds on the criterion of "finality" by exploring what is peculiar to man. Aristotle gives the reader two reasons why he is going to study the function: 1) everything has a function to perform, and 2) the goodness or the efficiency of everything is found in that function (*EN* I.7 1097b28). For example, every member of the human body has some function: the ear to hear, the hand to do things, and when this member of the body fulfills its function it is a good member of the body. So, Aristotle has to establish what the function of man is, and then, based on this he will be able to explain better what happiness is.

Aristotle explains the criterion of the function by looking at what is peculiar to humans (*EN* I.7 1098a1). What is peculiar to every human being is "the practical life of the rational part of man" (*EN* I.7 1098a3). The ability to exercise one's rational faculty is what Aristotle has in view when talks about rational life. Based on this explanation, the function of man is understood as the activity of the soul in conformity with rational principle (*EN* I.7 1098a20). When this activity is performed well and rightly, the good man is fulfilling his function. This is, in Aristotle's words, a "certain form of life" (*EN* I.7 1098a13). This metaphysical phrase, which has to be understood in the general Aristotelian framework of "matter" and "form" as the two elements of every particular thing, describes the identity or the defining character of every human being. When the faculties of the soul are active in accordance with the rational principle, the human being fulfills his/her function, and when these faculties are active in accordance with excellence (*EN* I.7 1098a20) s/he is fulfilling the function well. This is how the "good of man" is described by Aristotle with the help of the criterion of the function.

When Aristotle is finished with his exposition of the function criterion, he offers the reader a major signpost by saying: "let this account serve to describe the Good in outline" [περιγεγράφθω . . . τἀγαθὸν]. What is understood by this is described by the action of "making a rough sketch" (*EN* I.7 1098a21). I will explain in detail the significance of this signpost in 3.1.1 where I will argue that this phrase should be understood as a political educational metaphor: "perimeter of the good." Thus, these two distinct criteria of finality and function are used by Aristotle to delineate the "perimeter of the good."

2.2.4 The human goodness

Aristotle will continue to explore within this "perimeter of the good" examining the "nature of goodness." He has to do this because he defines happiness as the "activity of the soul in conformity with perfect goodness" (*EN* I.13 1102a5). For Aristotle, the goodness of humans is an "excellence of soul" (*EN* I.13 1102a25). This is the reason for which everyone who studies politics has to study the soul and its nature (*EN* I.13 1102a25).

Aristotle presents his understanding of the soul as having two parts ("irrational" and "capable of reason," *EN* I.13 1102a30), and of virtue as depending on this understanding of the soul: moral and intellectual (*EN* I.13 1103a5). These two kinds of virtue, moral and intellectual, are studied further and Aristotle says that we, as humans, have the natural ability to develop them, and by habit we develop this ability to maturity (*EN* II.1 1103a25). This capacity "given by nature" is understood by Aristotle in metaphysical terms. We have these capacities "in a potential form" and we are able to exercise them (*EN* II.1 1103a30). This is how, in the area of virtue, a human can move from potentiality to actuality; this is the basic framework of change in Aristotelian metaphysics. When we exercise them, we become more virtuous: "we become just by doing just acts" (*EN* II.1 1103b30). In other words, certain activities form certain moral dispositions (*EN* II.1 1103b15).

This relationship between activities and moral dispositions makes Aristotle to inquire into the area of conduct (*EN* II.2 1103b30). His analysis is detailed (see *EN* II.2 1103b30–1104b1) and reaches the following conclusion: when we observe the mean [relative to us] we have a stable disposition of our mind and this is a virtue (*EN* II.6 1107a1). We will position ourselves between all kind of excesses; I will explain the way of the moderation in 4.2.6. In Book II of *EN* Aristotle shows the relevance of "virtue" to his study of happiness. He will expand his inquiry of virtues extensively for several other books, but in Book X he returns to his inquiry of happiness. This is what I will explain in the next section.

2.2.5 Contemplation

The way he returns to the topic of happiness is worth mentioning, because he uses the phrase: εὐδαιμονία τύπῳ ("type of happiness" or "imprint of happiness," my translation; *EN* X.6 1176a30). He used this kind of formulas with "type" in Books I and II. He chooses the language of τύπος ("type") to continue his inquiry. His exposition in Book X.6–9 is the completion of his "function" argument. The completion of the "function" argument is accomplished in the following way: "if happiness consists in activity in accordance with virtue, it is reasonable that it should be activity in accordance with the highest virtue; and this will be the virtue of the best part of us" (*EN* X.7 1177a15). The highest virtue as the virtue of the best part of us is the ultimate point in his inquiry into the function of man; it is the best of the best part of us.

Analyzing the activity of the best part of us helps Aristotle to complete his inquiry on happiness. Aristotle identifies the best part of us as being the part that rules, leads, and gives us knowledge of what is noble and divine (*EN* X.7 1177a15). That part is our intellect. The reference to those elements (rule, lead, knowledge of noble and divine) can be understood to help Aristotle to reach the ultimate goal of his inquiry. Every human needs the right rule of reason, the practice of what is noble, and to reach the highest possible stage of his/her actuality. And in Aristotle's metaphysics, as I will argue later in 4.1.2, this has to do with divinity, the unmoved mover. God, the unmoved mover is the pure actuality in Aristotle's worldview, it is the supreme final aim of everything.

This best part of us, the intellect, has its own proper activity, and when this is done in accordance with its proper virtue or excellence, this activity is the activity of contemplation (*EN* X.7 1177a20). This reference to "contemplation" is not new because Aristotle already mentioned it (I.10 1100b20, IV.2 1122b17, VII.3 1146b14).

The fact that in Book X Aristotle identifies happiness with contemplation is not a different approach to that of Books I and II on this subject, but one that is in agreement with the results already accomplished; I will argue in favor of this interpretation in 5.2. Also, Aristotle says, it is in agreement with the truth (*EN* X.7 1177a20). The intellect being the highest thing in us, its activity, contemplation, is the highest activity. Aristotle understands contemplation as being continuous, pleasant, self-sufficient, and loved for its own sake; that is why it constitutes "complete human happiness" (*EN* X.7 1177b25).

Contemplation is a life at a higher level because it is the activity of the intellect, which, according to Aristotle, is the divine part of us (*EN* X.7 1177b30). This affirmation about the life of contemplation as being "higher than human level" has to be explained carefully. It does not mean that it is beyond our reach as humans, but rather that because of the divine element within us, which is our intellect, we, as humans, are able to live higher than human level, we are able to contemplate. This is a life that is not lived at the level of physical needs, but a life lived at the level of our intellect, which is the "highest thing in us." Our "composite nature" (human/divine) leads to this differentiation between the life of the intellect and the life of the human being (*EN* X.7 1177b30).

In *EN* X.7 1178a5 there is another strong indication that here, in Book X, Aristotle continues his "function" criterion: "that which is best and most pleasant for each creature is that which is proper to the nature of each." This link between "what is best" and "that which is proper to the nature of each" is explored further by Aristotle. The life of the best part of us which is the life of the intellect is the "best and the pleasant life" for us, humans (*EN* X.7 1178a5). In comparison with this best and most pleasant life, the virtuous moral life is happy only "in a secondary degree" (*EN* X.8 1178a10). This affirmation means that any virtue that is not intellectual does not reach the highest point. Aristotle makes this distinction based on the way he explains the nature of the soul. When the intellect does not act in a central way, that activity will be a moral activity and it will constitute happiness, but in a secondary degree. It is "secondary" because it does not reach the highest possible point for humans. This highest, ultimate point is reached when the intellect, which is the highest thing in us, is active, when it contemplates. I will argue for this interpretation in 5.2.3.

Towards the end of his inquiry Aristotle discusses the role of the "external equipment" in his understanding of happiness. He says that there is "little need" of it (*EN* X.8 1178a25). Aristotle approaches the role of the external goods in relation to happiness by observing that our human nature "is not self-sufficient for contemplation." The person who contemplates, the philosopher, is a human being with physical needs such as "health," "food," and other "requirements" (*EN* X.8 1179a1). These basic needs have to be covered to sustain physical life.

The last major signpost is in *EN* X.9 1179a35 where Aristotle says that "we have sufficiently discussed in their outlines [τοῖς τύποις] the subjects of Happiness and of Virtue in its various forms, and also Friendship and Pleasure may we assume that the investigation we proposed is now complete?" This usage of τύπος at the end of the inquiry completes the giant ring composition started at the beginning of the inquiry in *EN* I.2 1094a25: "we ought to make any attempt to determine at all events in outline [τύπῳ] what exactly this Supreme Good is." Thus, as I will argue in 3.1.2, what Aristotle does in his whole inquiry in *EN* is to give the reader his understanding of the "τύπος (type/imprint) of happiness" (*EN* X.6 1175b30). The full argument for translating and interpreting Aristotle in this way will be given in 3.1.2.

2.2.6 Conclusion

Thus, the overall structure of Aristotle's inquiry is given by several key phrases. 1. The first major signpost is at *EN* I.7 1098a21 where Aristotle tells the reader what happened so far into his inquiry. What has been argued for is described as a "perimeter of the good" [περιγεγράφθω τἀγαθὸν]. This perimeter was delineated by Aristotle with the help of two criteria: finality and function. The criterion of finality [τέλος] is about εὐδαιμονία as being the ultimate end, the good of the state, the end in itself, and self-sufficient. The criterion of the function [ἔργον ἀνθρωπόυ] builds upon the criterion of finality by exploring what is peculiar to man; the goodness or the efficiency of everything is found in its function. The "function of man" is the activity/actuality of the soul in conformity with rational principle. Within this delineated perimeter Aristotle studies εὐδαιμονία.

2. At the beginning (*EN* I.2 1094a25) and at the end (*EN* X.9 1179b1) of the inquiry, Aristotle uses τύπος/type/imprint as the main lens to understand his study about εὐδαιμονία. The "type/imprint of happiness" directs the reader towards an understanding of it in terms of formation, and practice. This constitutes the major hermeneutical key to interpret the concept of εὐδαιμονία in *EN*, it is an educational, formative concept.

That is why my general observation about how to study Aristotle's inquiry about εὐδαιμονία is to listen to these two main phrases: "perimeter of the good" and "imprint of happiness." To inquire about εὐδαιμονία the reader needs to delineate a perimeter with the help of criteria of finality and function, and then, within this perimeter, s/he can come with an understanding of εὐδαιμονία that can be formed in his/her life.

But this study of mine is one among many other studies about εὐδαιμονία in *EN*. Other researchers before me have studied this topic in various ways. I need to see how they have approached the subject.

The vast majority of all research done on happiness in *EN* focuses on three main areas or questions.

1) What type of good happiness is? There are two main camps: those who say that happiness is a monistic good, and others who say that happiness is a composite good.

2) What is the relationship between happiness and complete happiness? Is Aristotle working with one conception of happiness or two? Is his inquiry coherent or not?

3) What is the relationship between happiness and the external goods? Is there a need for possessions and wealth to attain happiness? Can happiness be "ruined" by the loss of the external goods?

Every major scholarly study on happiness discusses these questions. They have captured the debates about how Aristotle understands εὐδαιμονία in that these questions are focused on to the exclusion of other possible questions, and other questions are neglected or ignored. In the next section, I will present and analyze the major ideas of different scholars who give different answers to these important questions. I will present these positions/ answers, and then, I will evaluate them critically.

2.3 THE QUESTIONS OF THE DEBATES AND CRITICISM

This section is intended to offer an analysis of the major answers given to the three important questions about happiness in *EN*.[7] In 2.3.1, I will study the first important question "What type of good is happiness?" There are two major answers to this question given by scholars: a composite good or a dominant good. I will argue that these answers do not reflect entirely what Aristotle says about εὐδαιμονία in *EN*, and that the interpreter needs to focus somewhere else, namely, towards εὐδαιμονία as ἐνεργεία, which in Aristotle's worldview means happiness as actuality.

Then, in 2.3.2, I will analyze the second important question: "Are there one or two accounts of εὐδαιμονία?" There are two principal answers to this question the scholarly debates: Aristotle works with one account or

---

7. For other recent analyses of the scholarly debates on happiness in *EN*, see May, *Ethics*, 1–17; Russell, *Happiness*, 13–35. The scholarly literature on the meaning of εὐδαιμονία in *EN* is growing all the time. The most recent academic titles include: Chang, "Happiness"; Lawrence, "Human Function"; Bartlett, "Happiness"; Caesar, "Happiness"; Meyer, "Ultimate End"; Long, "Eudaimonia"; Dahl, "Contemplation"; Reeve, *Action*; and Roche, "External Goods."

Aristotle works with two accounts of happiness in *EN*. I will argue that in *EN*, Aristotle works with one account of happiness.

In 2.3.3 I will analyze the debate about "Happiness and external goods." The debated aspects are those related to what happens to happiness when the external goods are lost, and what the nature of the relationship between external goods and virtues is. The answers given by various scholars say that human goodness is fragile, and the loss of external goods can affect happiness, and that the external goods are the external product of our virtuous actions. I will argue that εὐδαιμονία is stable enough and that it cannot be dislodged easily, and that the external goods are needed not because εὐδαιμονία needs them, but that our human nature, which is not self-sufficient, needs them for our existence.

2.3.1 What type of good is happiness?

Happiness as the good of man has been understood either as a composite good (this view is also known the "inclusive" interpretation) or as a dominant/monistic good. In this subsection, I will present the debate that has been going for a long time, between these two main interpretations of εὐδαιμονία. The key terms "inclusive" and "dominant/monistic" try to describe the nature of εὐδαιμονία. Εὐδαιμονία as the ultimate good of man is an end that includes all the ends of our endeavors ("inclusive" interpretation) or εὐδαιμονία is a dominant end towards which all other ends point, and these are subordinated to it ("dominant/monistic" interpretation). I have selected representative scholars from these two camps (J. L. Ackrill, R. Kraut, and others), and will evaluate their positions, offering objections to both interpretations by arguing that εὐδαιμονία, in *EN*, is better interpreted as actuality/ἐνεργεία.

The understanding of happiness as a composite good is explained as follows. Aristotle says that happiness is the ultimate unifying end for the sake of which humans perform all their good actions.[8] When some actions are done for the sake of happiness, the phrase "for the sake of" is understood in "constituent" terms. These good actions, which are ends in themselves, are "constituent" to happiness.[9] As an analogy, a cup of coffee is a good item for so many of us. But this good item is a composite good. The constitutive items of it are: water, coffee extract, temperature, pressure, and

---

8. Annas, "Aristotle on Virtue and Happiness," 36.

9. Ackrill, "*Eudaimonia*," 72; Irwin, "Permanent Happiness," 10.

(for some) sugar. When all these are combined together in various ways and proportions we obtain a desired, good item: the cup of coffee.

The good actions performed by humans are worth doing and they all together are the content of the best and most desired kind of life, happiness.[10] This composite understanding of happiness offers a particular explanation of the finality and self-sufficiency of happiness. Because happiness "includes" in itself good and desirable actions it is final and self-sufficient. The best there is, it is included in itself; that is why it is final and self-sufficient.[11] Because of this inclusion of all ends,[12] happiness is sought for its own sake, and not for the sake of something else.[13] This is how happiness is the ultimate aim of the science of politics. In this architectonic structure of the ultimate political end, all other ends are "embraced" (*EN* 1094b6–7).[14] In a city, the ends of the sciences and of various parts of government are all constituent elements of the good of the state. The science of education will have its end of educated, mature people who do their part for the good of the state. The economy, the army, and all other endeavors will have their ends as constitutive of the ultimate good of the state.

The understanding of happiness as a monistic good (also known as the "dominant" interpretation) is explained as follows. The final hierarchical end, for Aristotle, is not an inclusive aggregate but "one type of good."[15] Aristotle's definition of happiness based on the function argument speaks about one activity of the soul in accordance with virtue, not about an aggregate composed of several actions, virtues, and people.[16] These are goods in themselves but the problem with them is that they are not final enough.[17] Virtuous activity is the good of man, and this is one single item, not a composed variety of goods. By virtuous activity Aristotle means the virtuous activity of the soul, not a vast array of activities in the city, which have their own contribution to a superior end.

10. Ackrill, "*Eudaimonia*," 63; Pakaluk, *Nicomachean Ethics*, 319.

11. Gomez-Lobo, "The Ergon Inference," 183.

12. Höffe, *Aristotle*, 151.

13. Ackrill, "*Eudaimonia*," 65.

14. Ackrill, "*Eudaimonia*," 68; Urmson, *Aristotle's Ethics*, 119; Hester, "Function of Man," 12.

15. Kraut, "Human Good," 79; Kenny, "Happiness," 100; Richardson Lear, "Structure of Ends," 397; Hardie, "Final Good," 283.

16. Kraut, "Human Good," 81; Bush, "Happiness," 50.

17. Richardson Lear, "Happiness," 398.

Aristotle does not add to this activity anything else; happiness for Aristotle is not a state, but an activity only.[18] Virtuous activity as the good of man is not a good among other goods, but the good for the sake of which everything else is done. This virtuous activity of the soul is sustained by other goods (health, people, etc.) but these goods do not add value to it.[19] The end of Aristotle's inquiry identifies this one good as contemplation, the virtuous activity of the rational soul. This is the highest good because is the activity of the highest part of us, our intellect.[20]

These are the main points of the debate that started in the 1960s and there is no agreed consensus. Sometimes these two sides do not represent each other in a precise way. For example, the dominant interpretation does not picture the inclusive position exactly as Ackrill presented it. Kraut uses the metaphor of "aggregate" which suggests "a whole formed by combining several (typically disparate) elements" (*New Oxford American Dictionary*). But Ackrill does not use this image to describe his understanding of the inclusiveness of happiness. He explicitly mentions that in *EN* Aristotle does not use the language of "parts and whole"[21] as he does in *Eudemian Ethics* 1219a35–9. Also, Ackrill does not use the language of "all-inclusive" as Kraut describes his position. Instead, Ackrill speaks about happiness as "the life that contains all intrinsically worthwhile activities."[22] My observation is that when we analyze the "inclusive" position, the "intrinsicality" of happiness and the focus on "activities" have to be front-line. For Ackrill and the inclusive interpreters these "worthwhile activities" are part of happiness in an essential way, not as "parts of a whole." The focus of their investigation is not so much on "one" activity but on several activities whose ends are ultimately included in the final aim, which is εὐδαιμονία.

Ackrill and the "inclusive" interpretation is understood correctly if the interpreter stays close to Ackrill's main affirmation about the meaning of the phrase "A for the sake of B." For Ackrill, this means that "A contributes as a constituent to B." Ackrill and the "inclusive" interpreters do not understand it to mean "A is a means to subsequent B." When this aspect is central (a constituent of an end *versus* a means towards something subsequent), we can see exactly the major difference between the "inclusive" and "monistic"

---

18. Kraut, "Human Good," 82.

19. Kraut, "Human Good," 85; Kenny, *Ethics*, 204.

20. Kraut, "Human Good," 88; Richardson, "Happy Lives," 7.

21 Ackrill, "*Eudaimonia*," 70.

22. Ackrill, "*Eudaimonia*," 63.

interpretations of happiness. The dominant/monistic interpretation shows the reader that when Aristotle reaches the function argument, he speaks about just one activity, which is "the activity of the rational soul in accordance with virtue."

There are scholars like Bush, whose position I will present in 5.3, who argue that because there is no agreed consensus, and neither of these two positions can answer the important question of the relation between human and divine happiness,[23] we should look in other places for a way forward to understand Aristotle's understanding of εὐδαιμονία. I agree with Bush that the inclusive/dominant debate has gone on for too long without an agreed solution and that we need to come with different answers.

These two interpretations can be criticized at a deeper level. First, we should let Aristotle speak for himself. Aristotle does not use the language of "inclusive" or "dominant/monisitic" to describe the ultimate good. Ackrill acknowledges that Aristotle does not use explicitly the language of "parts of a whole" or "inclusion."[24] But Aristotle does not use the language of "monistic" or "dominant" end either. Instead he speaks about εὐδαιμονία as τέλος (end, ultimate end), and he speaks about εὐδαιμονία as ἔργον ἀνθρώπου (function of man). My observation is that the interpreter has to listen and follow the lead of Aristotle. Aristotle explains what he is doing in relation to εὐδαιμονία by using two important metaphors in his two major signposts at I.7 1098a17 and X.6 1176a31: περιγράφω and τύπος, "to draw a line around something/to delineate a perimeter" and "to blow a form/an imprint." The criteria of finality and function establish the perimeter of εὐδαιμονία, and at the end of the inquiry Aristotle accomplishes a "type/imprint" of εὐδαιμονία. As I will argue in the next chapter these insights are the major contribution to knowledge brought by this project. The main thing that Aristotle does from I.1 to I.7 is not to establish whether εὐδαιμονία is "inclusive" or "monistic," but to establish the "perimeter" within which he can make affirmations about it.

Second, the interpreters in both camps do not provide Aristotelian arguments to argue for either the "inclusive" or the "monistic" understanding of εὐδαιμονία. By this objection I mean the following aspects: for example, neither Ackrill and Kraut offers the reader an explanation of what a τέλος is in Aristotle's view. I am not saying that Ackrill and Kraut do not know what a τέλος is for Aristotle, but that they do not use that knowledge to interpret

---

23. Bush, "Happiness," 49–51.
24. Ackrill, "*Eudaimonia*," 72.

εὐδαιμονία as τέλος, which is the first definition of εὐδαιμονία in *EN*. Both Ackrill and Kraut try to explain the meaning of the affirmation "A for the sake of B," but not in Aristotelian terms. I know that this objection is hard, but I make it respectfully.

To understand the ultimate τέλος in Aristotle's worldview is not so much to debate about several components or one single end, but, as I will argue later in 4.2.2, the τέλος, in Aristotle's worldview, is ultimately about god, the pure actuality, the ultimate aim of every potentiality. This observation rearranges the whole analysis of the meaning of εὐδαιμονία as the ultimate end/τέλος in Aristotle's ethics, because the focus is no longer on the *composed* end versus the *dominant* end, but on the *ultimate* end which, for Aristotle, is the ultimate pure actuality. Εὐδαιμονία is no longer understood as a composite good or as a dominant good, but as the ultimate actuality in which every potentiality reaches its end. I will present the whole argument for this interpretation in Chapters 4 and 5, which constitute the main content of my thesis.

In *EN* Books I and II Aristotle speaks about εὐδαιμονία, but in Book X he uses the phrase ἡ τελεία εὐδαιμονία. This fact leads to the second important question the scholars ask: Do we have a single account of happiness or there are two distinct ones in *EN*? In the next section I will present and analyze this second major question of the larger debate on εὐδαιμονία.

2.3.2 One or two accounts of εὐδαιμονία?

In this subsection I will present the two answers to this important question. The camp who argues for two accounts, one in Book I and II, and the other in Book X, will be represented by Nagel as the main interlocutor, and the camp who argue for one account throughout the entire *EN* will be represented by Hardie. Then, I will present my critical analysis of them.

I will analyze Nagel's position, who describes Aristotle as not being sure who we are, and this fact makes him go at different times in different directions. We as humans are close both to animals and to gods. We are concerned both with things related to everyday life and with things higher than ourselves. Then, I will analyze Hardie's position, who argues that Aristotle's understanding of εὐδαιμονία as a monolithic end is coherent throughout the inquiry in *EN*.

For most part of his inquiry about happiness, Aristotle speaks only about εὐδαιμονία (Books I and II), but in Book X.7 he uses the phrase "perfect/complete happiness" [ἡ τελεία εὐδαιμονία]. Is he speaking about the same thing or about something else? The answers to this question found in the scholarly literature are two: Aristotle is consistent and offers a single account of εὐδαιμονία throughout his entire inquiry in *EN*[25] or Aristotle works with two accounts of εὐδαιμονία in his inquiry.[26] The answers given to the first major question (what type of good εὐδαιμονία is?) tends to position scholars on a certain side in relation to this second major question: usually the "inclusivist" scholars tend to argue for two accounts of εὐδαιμονία in *EN*, and the "dominant/monistic" scholars tend to argue for one account of εὐδαιμονία in *EN*.

The scholars who argue for two accounts of εὐδαιμονία speak about Aristotle's undecidedness between the two accounts he tries to keep together: a "comprehensive" and an "intellectualist" understanding of εὐδαιμονία.[27] From the various types of answers which argue for two accounts of εὐδαιμονία, I present and analyze the representative answer provided by Thomas Nagel.

According to Nagel, Aristotle shows tendencies in both these directions. There is this "ambivalence" between these two accounts of εὐδαιμονία because Aristotle "is not sure who we are."[28] When Aristotle presents his "function" argument (*EN* I.7 1097b25–1098a20), the humans are understood in different ways: they have particularities that go in two directions: "of gods and dogs."[29] Humans are able to exhibit various types of activities including consciousness and the basic life functions.[30]

This "conjunctive" understanding of humans is then rejected by Aristotle (*EN* I.7 1098a1–4) because a human being is a "complex organism" which functions at various supporting levels.[31] In relation to an animal, a human being is differentiated by his/her ability to reason, and the entire body through its functions supports this rational activity. Thus, in the human person, reason is supported by the functions of the body, and reason

25. Cooper, *Reason*, 235; Kraut, *Human Good*, 314; Kraut, "Human Good," 90; Van Cleemput, "Happiness," 95; Baracchi, *First Philosophy*, 96; Richardson Lear, "Happiness," 401.

26. Curzer, "Criteria," 422; Bush, "Happiness," 51; Shields, *Aristotle*, 341, 343; Curzer, *Virtues*, 392, 424; Nagel, "*Eudaimonia*," 252.

27. Nagel, "*Eudaimonia*," 252.

28. Nagel, "*Eudaimonia*," 253.

29. Nagel, "*Eudaimonia*," 255.

30. Nagel, "*Eudaimonia*," 256.

31. Nagel, "*Eudaimonia*," 256.

is not under the control of any lower function. This dominion of reason in the human body makes Aristotle to be inclined towards an intellectualist understanding of εὐδαιμονία[32] (EN VI.7 1141a21–3). This dominance of reason makes a "conjunction" understanding of the human person very unlikely. That is why according to an intellectualist interpretation, εὐδαιμονία is to be measured in terms of reason.

Nagel goes on to argue that this intellectualist situation is seen in another way when the practical life of humans is analyzed. Reason supports the everyday practical life of humans but has the ability to go beyond it.[33] Because of this, every human can transcend the concerns of everyday life and the concerns of society. This intellectualist position is strengthened in Book X.7–8. Aristotle is not sure how to describe the result of his inquiry, if it should be portrayed as "strictly human good."[34] Life is "higher than human," because the human beings have "something divine" in them. But, according to Nagel, this divine part of us has to be seen as "the highest aspect of our souls," and this makes it linked to "lowlier matters."[35] But this should not stop us to refine or cultivate our ability to transcend everything. We, as humans, have the ability to transcend ourselves, and ultimately become like gods; this ability to transcend everything makes us able to achieve εὐδαιμονία.[36]

Thus, this is how Nagel describes his interpretation of Aristotle where Aristotle is unsure who we are. The two major tendencies, towards gods or towards dogs are in focus at different times in Aristotle's inquiry. The ability of every human to transcend the everyday life leads Aristotle to end up his inquiry by focusing on an intellectualist understanding of happiness.

Against this understanding of Aristotle's indecision, between the two accounts of εὐδαιμονία in EN, there is the position that argues for a consistent answer to the question about what kind of life is the best. This argument for a coherent account of εὐδαιμονία states that, in EN, εὐδαιμονία is a monolithic end, which means that it includes theoretical activities.[37] In EN I, Aristotle gives us a "preliminary sketch,"[38] and later he will consider the

32. Nagel, "*Eudaimonia*," 257.
33. Nagel, "*Eudaimonia*," 257.
34. Nagel, "*Eudaimonia*," 258.
35. Nagel, "*Eudaimonia*," 258.
36. Nagel, "*Eudaimonia*," 259.
37. Hardie, "Best Life," 42.
38. Hardie, "Best Life," 35.

"theoretic life" even if he will not be specific about the virtues, namely, if he means one or several, and the best of them will remain unnamed.[39] The final end, εὐδαιμονία, as the political end is "a paramount object."[40] This final end, the good of man, includes both theoretical activities in Book I, and non-theoretical activities in Books VI and X. Hardie's position is the classical dominant/paramount understanding of εὐδαιμονία. The virtuous activities and the intellectual activities (study, contemplation) constitute the εὐδαιμονία.

But the "intellectualist" focus of Book X on εὐδαιμονία is not understood as a dedication to metaphysics that is separate from a life of virtues lived in the city.[41] The ability to think of every human being leads, according to Hardie, to a life in which "theory is paramount" and this makes happiness possible.[42] Thus, Hardie keeps together Aristotle's inquiry into one account of εὐδαιμονία. The intellectualist aim constitutes happiness at individual level and at the level of the whole city. Virtuous intellectual activity is the dominant end of humans in the city.

This second major question in the debate on εὐδαιμονία is about the relationship between the inquiry in *EN* I and *EN* X, especially between the terms "happiness" [εὐδαιμονία] and "perfect/complete happiness" [ἡ τελεία εὐδαιμονία]. Do we have two accounts of εὐδαιμονία or one? My answer is that between the two there is continuity towards completion. My main point is that this continuity towards completion is based on Aristotle's metaphysical teleology and not on a debatable lack of knowledge on Aristotle's part of what we are as humans, as Nagel says. I will present the details of my interpretation in 5.2.

I disagree with Nagel when he says that Aristotle is "not sure who we are," and because of this, he is undecided which account of εὐδαιμονία has to be embraced. Aristotle has a vast knowledge of the human soul which is the focus of his exploration of the human good, and this anthropological knowledge is integrated within a teleological perspective. That is why I argue that the overall major starting point of Aristotle's ethical inquiry is teleology, not anthropology. According to Aristotle, everything we enterprise aims towards some goal/end.

---

39. Hardie, "Best Life," 36.
40. Hardie, "Best Life," 42.
41. Hardie, "Best Life," 43, 44.
42. Hardie, "Best Life," 44.

The "function" argument does not add to the confusion, as Nagel suggests when he, sarcastically, says that we, the humans, have "a conjunctive *ergon* which overlaps the *erga* of gods and dogs."[43] According to Aristotle, human beings are complex beings and have a divine element in them, and the "function" argument is brought into inquiry because it is thought that it can help to acquire a better understanding of εὐδαιμονία. The "function" argument helps Aristotle to focus on what can help the inquirer to provide a more detailed account of εὐδαιμονία, and it shows how the "good of man" is identified. Later, in *EN* X.7, the "function" argument will continue to be used to identify the "highest virtue," which is the virtue of the "highest thing in us."

I agree with Nagel that "the divine part of us has to be seen as the highest aspect of our soul," and I interpret this in favor of Aristotle's overall anthropology; he knows many things about us humans. Nagel allows metaphysics to play an important role in understanding what Aristotle has to say about εὐδαιμονία. I also agree with Nagel that ultimately it is because humans have the "capacity to transcend themselves" that "they are capable of *eudaimonia*." I agree with this statement because in this activity of getting closer and more like to the gods, we get closer of achieving our actuality. Without this ability to transcend ourselves we are not able to achieve εὐδαιμονία.

Thus, the debate between one or two accounts of εὐδαιμονία focuses either on the ambivalence or indecision of Aristotle in relation to how to understand the human person, or on the consistency or coherence of Aristotle's understanding of εὐδαιμονία as a monolithic good. I am in the camp of those scholars who argue for a coherent understanding of εὐδαιμονία in EN, and I will argue in Chapters 4 and 5 that this coherent understanding is accomplished by delineating a clear perimeter of the good, and within this perimeter, εὐδαιμονία can be formed in peoples' lives. Now, I will present the third major question in the debates about εὐδαιμονία in *EN*, and that is about its relationship to the external goods.

2.3.3 Happiness and the external goods

The unknowns of life have an impact on εὐδαιμονία. For example, when a disaster strikes, and members of the family are lost, and property is destroyed, εὐδαιμονία is affected. The debated question is this: Is this impact

43. Nagel, *"Eudaimonia,"* 255.

decisive or partial? Can εὐδαιμονία be damaged or even destroyed? The answers are varied. What is Aristotle's answer to this question? The scholars[44] are divided in how they understand Aristotle on this subject. I selected Nussbaum and Cooper as the main interlocutors because of their importance and high profile in the Aristotelian studies. Later, in 5.5, I will add Annas to the debate.

So, in this section, I will consider Nussbaum and Cooper's positions. Nussbaum's position is that εὐδαιμονία has to be understood as ἐνεργεία, based on *Metaphysics* IX, as a complete activity. Nussbaum focus is on the stability of virtuous character, and this makes εὐδαιμονία hard to be dislodged. Cooper's position is that the external goods are products of our virtuous actions. Cooper understands the external goods as a component of εὐδαιμονία. I will criticize both these positions, arguing that a better understanding of this relationship between εὐδαιμονία and the external goods starts by focusing on the lack of our self-sufficiency. We need the external goods for our life, but εὐδαιμονία, which is self-sufficient does not. That is why the good character remains in place even when the external goods are lost because of disaster or a cataclysmic event.

Nussbaum's approach on the relationship between εὐδαιμονία and external goods focuses on "activity and disaster."[45] Nussbaum identifies the particularities of Aristotle's choice of speaking about εὐδαιμονία as "an activity," as *Metaphysics* IX tells us, and the destructive power of disaster and how εὐδαιμονία is able to survive even the worst of them.[46] That is why this position is labeled "proto-Stoic," which means that not even the worst events have the ability to affect the virtuous person, and this "Stoic" position, Nussbaum says, was uphold by Aristotle long before the Stoics. Thus, Nussbaum, in the light of *Metaphysics* IX, understands εὐδαιμονία as "activity/*energeia*" to mean that "*energeiai* are activities that are complete at any moment. They have their form in themselves."[47] This metaphysical understanding of εὐδαιμονία as an activity is fundamental for Nussbaum when she asks: "Is *eudaimonia* vulnerable? How far can it resist against disaster?"[48]

---

44. Roche, "External Goods," 37–38.
45. Nussbaum, *Fragility*, 318.
46. Irwin, "Permanent Happiness," 7.
47. Nussbaum, *Fragility*, 326.
48. Nussbaum, *Fragility*, 318.

According to Nussbaum, Aristotle mentions two ways of understanding the relationship between good life and chance. 1) The good life is about "activities that are maximally stable and invulnerable to chance." 2) Good living and "actual activity according to excellence" are distinct, and based on this, when someone is in a virtuous condition, that is enough for εὐδαιμονία.[49] According to Nussbaum, Aristotle's argument is a combination of these two.[50] This combination is seen in the fact that εὐδαιμονία, on the one hand, requires "actual activity" to reach its intended aim/end, and on the other hand, disaster can disrupt good activity. Every good action can be affected decisively by luck. Because there is a distinction between "being good" and "living well" when disaster strikes, and the good life is gone, even the virtuous state/being good is impacted.[51] This state of "being good" is understood by Nussbaum as the condition at which someone arrives by moving from mere potentiality. "Being good" is the flourishing of someone's potentiality.[52]

But this activity according to excellence operates properly in certain conditions, it needs resources, good health, and a particular social context.[53] When someone is tortured "on the wheel" s/he cannot act justly. Εὐδαιμονία as an activity is vulnerable and it can be impeded. There are various ways in which actions that are beyond our control can interfere with εὐδαιμονία.[54]

A test case for εὐδαιμονία, as Aristotle understands it, is the story of King Priam (Aristotle mentions the misfortunes of King Priam in *EN* I.9 1100a5–9). The loss of the Troy's war and the death of his sons did not destroy the quality of the king's life, because all the way to the end, King Priam showed good character through his actions,[55] even when Achille's son kills him. The virtues of character are stable dispositions and the dislodging of someone from these is a rare event, even when the conditions of the living well are destroyed. The good life can be taken away by disaster, but rarely the good character.[56] The damage done by disaster can be resisted by "good

49. Nussbaum, *Fragility*, 319, 320.

50. Nussbaum, *Fragility*, 322.

51. Nussbaum, *Fragility*, 322.

52. Nussbaum, *Fragility*, 324.

53. Nussbaum, *Fragility*, 325; Broadie, *Ethics*, 54.

54. Nussbaum, *Fragility*, 327.

55. Nussbaum, *Fragility*, 329.

56. Irwin, "Permanent Happiness," 7; Nussbaum, *Fragility*, 329.

character and practical wisdom"; character and wisdom will help that person to continue to "act nobly."[57]

Nussbaum's conclusion is that "an Aristotelian conception of *eudaimonia*, which bases excellent activity on stable goodness of character, makes the good life tolerably stable in the face of the world."[58] This conclusion focuses the study of εὐδαιμονία as ἐνεργεία on virtues of character. The completeness of εὐδαιμονία as ἐνεργεία makes it hard to be dislodged.

A different understanding of what Aristotle is saying about the relationship between εὐδαιμονία and the external goods is defended by Cooper.[59] According to Cooper, Aristotle understands "human flourishing" based on several factors: complete life, practice of human virtues, and sufficient external goods.[60] In the Hellenistic times, according to Cooper, *EN* was treated as an "authoritative text" when someone was looking for the Aristotelian position concerning the human good.[61] The goods needed by people are understood in a broader way and they include the goods of the body and the external goods of wealth, power, and friends.[62] But according to Cooper, the relationship between these goods and the human person has to be defined as exactly as possible: the external goods are the external products of our virtuous actions. When someone rightly achieves a particular possession, that possession, that is other than knowledge or virtue, will be an external good.[63]

When the external goods are destroyed or lost, "one's blessedness [is] disfigured."[64] This is so, because εὐδαιμονία needs a sufficient supply of goods for performing virtuous activities. Cooper acknowledges that this reason for the needs of external goods in the life of the virtuous and happy person is difficult to explain, but he understands it as pointing to how the virtuous actions are hindered if this person does not have them.[65] This

---

57. Nussbaum, *Fragility*, 333.

58. Nussbaum, *Fragility*, 334.

59. Cooper, "Goods of Fortune," 173–96.

60. Cooper, "Goods of Fortune," 174.

61. Cooper, "Goods of Fortune," 176.

62. Cooper, "Goods of Fortune," 177.

63. Cooper, "Goods of Fortune," 178; Shea, "Happiness," 83; Irwin, "Permanent Happiness," 6; Roche, "External Goods," 40.

64. Cooper, "Goods of Fortune," 180.

65. Cooper, "Goods of Fortune," 182.

explanation is obscure and in need for further clarification. Cooper offers the explanation as follows:

> One central context for the exercise of the virtues is in the raising of children and the subsequent common life one spends with them, once adult, in the morally productive common pursuit of morally significant ends. If this context is not realized in one's life then, Aristotle would be saying, one's virtuous activities are diminished and restricted.[66]

This is how, according to Cooper, Aristotle distinguishes between the instrumentality of the external goods and the contexts that are created by the existence of the external goods.[67] Thus, when someone has them, s/he can do a variety of virtuous activities, and when s/he does not have them his/her blessedness is marred.

Cooper considers that the external goods in Aristotle have to be seen as "goods of fortune" because someone either has them or not and that is dependent on luck.[68] No one has control over them. But the "goods of fortune" contribute to happiness of a person when this person reaps the effects these goods have on his/her future activities.[69]

This understanding of the role of the external goods is found, Cooper says, in the peripatetic tradition of Arius Didymus (beginning of first century AD), Aspasius (second century AD), and Alexander of Aphrodisias (second century AD).[70] All these ancient authors, according to Cooper confirm that Aristotle requires the "external goods as one element in *eudaimonia*."[71] A virtuous person knows the good use of any external goods in any circumstance (even in adversity). These peripatetic authors understand the role of the external goods in the same way. Virtues equip people to act morally in a wide variety of situations,[72] and will use whatever the external goods have at his/her disposal to the best possible. This is what the virtues essentially are: how the external goods are best used in any circumstance.[73]

---

66. Cooper, "Goods of Fortune," 183.

67. Cooper, "Goods of Fortune," 184.

68. Curzer, *Virtues*, 419.

69. Cooper, "Goods of Fortune," 184; Bush, "Happiness," 60.

70. Cooper, "Goods of Fortune," 185.

71. See the quoted examples in Cooper, "Goods of Fortune," 185–87.

72. Cooper, "Goods of Fortune," 187.

73. Cooper, "Goods of Fortune," 188.

Thus, according to Cooper, the external goods are integrated in εὐδαιμονία, and this means that their value is seen in how they contribute to the performed virtuous activity.[74] This insight is based on Aristotle's thought that the character of a human being is determined by what that person does.[75] So, according to Cooper, Aristotle goes beyond the role of instrumentality for the external goods in the life of the virtuous person, to that of them being "a second component of *eudaimonia*, alongside virtuous activity." This integrative understanding of the external goods as a component of εὐδαιμονία is based, according to Cooper, on the effect the external goods have upon how the virtuous human being continues to live his/her virtuous life.[76]

My analysis of these two interpretations of the role of the external goods is based on how Aristotle ends his inquiry in *EN* X.8 into the role they have in relation to εὐδαιμονία.

I disagree with both of these two interpretations on how the subject of external goods is approached in *EN*. The interpreter needs to listen all the way to the end what Aristotle has to say about this subject. When the whole picture is sketched the interpreter identifies the main hermeneutical perspective for understanding the question. I consider *EN* X.8 1178b34, where Aristotle tells the reader about "the why" of the external goods, as being decisive in this respect. Aristotle says that the philosopher needs the external goods because, being a human, his "φύσις (nature) is not self-sufficient." Εὐδαιμονία is self-sufficient, but the human person is not. That is why the external goods are needed. It is not that εὐδαιμονία needs the external goods, but that we as humans, for our own survival and activity, need them. My extended analysis of this subject is presented in 5.5.2.1.

I believe that Cooper's peripatetic interpretation of Aristotle does not reflect entirely what Aristotle says in *EN*. I agree that there is a link, in Aristotle's ethical thought in *EN*, between what a person performs and what that person is. Because of this, as Cooper says, there is a link between the external goods and εὐδαιμονία, but as an instrument through which a person performs noble activities, and by this performance that person becomes more virtuous. A person does not become more virtuous by having external goods. Actually, Aristotle says that the rich and the powerful do not perform more noble activities, but the person who has moderate

74. Cooper, "Goods of Fortune," 188.
75. Cooper, "Goods of Fortune," 195.
76. Cooper, "Goods of Fortune," 196.

external goods does (*EN* X.8 1179a9). The person who has goods in abundance tends to be stingy. The abundance of the external goods most likely is an impediment to εὐδαιμονία.

I am more in agreement with Nussbaum about the fact that the happy human being cannot be dislodged from his/her happiness. There is a strong element of "proto-Stoicism" in Aristotle when he argues for the stability of εὐδαιμονία.

But I disagree with Nussbaum that Aristotle uses εὐδαιμονία and μᾱκάριος interchangeably in *EN* I.8 1099b3 where he says that the lack of external goods "mars our blessedness" [ῥυπαίνουσι τὸ μακάριον]. There is no complete synonymy between two words, and we should try to understand why Aristotle choose to use μᾱκάριος instead of εὐδαιμονία. Aristotle gives us the difference in meaning between these two terms in *EN* I.10 1101a15–22 where he says about εὐδαιμονία that it is "an end, something utterly and absolutely final and complete," and about μᾱκάριος, that it is the person who possesses good things as being "supremely blessed [. . .] on the human scale of bliss." This blessedness can be marred, but εὐδαιμονία cannot. But because our human φύσις is not self-sufficient, we need external goods of "food, health, and other requirements."

Thus, εὐδαιμονία as such is self-sufficient, but we as human beings are not. That is why we need external goods. The external goods help us to perform noble acts, and this performance of them help us to become more virtuous persons. But the existence of the external goods does not guarantee εὐδαιμονία. A rich person does not necessarily reach εὐδαιμονία. On the contrary, a rich person tends to be ungenerous. The external goods, in this case, are an impediment for εὐδαιμονία.

2.4 CONCLUSION

This overview of Aristotle's inquiry about εὐδαιμονία in *EN* shows what are the main phrases that should be explained by the interpreter. Aristotle's main signposts give the reader the needed help to understand what Aristotle does in *EN* concerning the meaning of εὐδαιμονία. The fact that the entire inquiry has to be seen as an inquiry towards a particular understanding of εὐδαιμονία as a "type/imprint" of happiness (*EN* X.6 1176a30, X.9 1179b1) says that εὐδαιμονία is to be formed into people's lives, and this "imprint" is blown into a clearly delineated "perimeter" (*EN* I.7 1098a21).

The delineation of the perimeter of the good is the main thing Aristotle does in *EN* I.1–7; he does not try to establish whether εὐδαιμονία is inclusive or monistic. The reader needs to explore the meaning of τέλος in relation to εὐδαμονία. Τέλος is an essential aspect of Aristotle's metaphysics, politics, and virtue. The ultimate end in Aristotle's worldview is the unmovable substance, god as νοῦς, the pure actuality of the whole universe. Εὐδαιμονία as τέλος points in the direction of this ultimate end of everything, towards god. We do not have a discussion about whether the εὐδαιμονία is a composite or dominant good, but what we have is an inquiry about εὐδαιμονία as the ultimate actuality of every human being. Ultimately εὐδαιμονία is the end of the movement from potentiality to actuality, it is a metaphysical teleological good.

This is confirmed when Aristotle analyses it with the help of function. For Aristotle, the function of something gives it the reason to be, and the final cause is the function it fulfills. The final cause is the unmovable substance, god, and becoming more like it/him is to fulfill the function of man. The rational virtuous activity of the soul is the best of humanity, is the function we have. Reaching the completion of this function is by focusing upon the highest virtue of the highest part of us, upon the actuality of our νοῦς.

The three questions from above analysis are important, but they should not have the precedence they have. The reason for this is the fact that the interpreter of Aristotle needs to follow him in his inquiry and to listen to what Aristotle tells his audience that he is doing. As I pointed out above, Aristotle speaks about the nature of εὐδαιμονία, and he reaches the last stage of ἡ τέλεια εὐδαιμονία in his inquiry, and he discusses the need for the external goods, but, respectfully, these three mentioned questions are not the major points of Aristotle's inquiry.

That is why I propose a method that focuses not on various questions the interpreter might have, but on the summaries of Aristotle himself (*EN* I.7 1098a21–24 and X.6 1176a30–33) in which he tells the reader explicitly what he has done. This new reading of εὐδαιμονία is presented in the next chapter.

CHAPTER 3

A NEW READING OF ARISTOTLE'S ETHICAL INQUIRY ABOUT HAPPINESS

3.1 INTRODUCTION

So far, the major point I made in this book is that Aristotle, in *EN*, describes his inquiry into the meaning of εὐδαιμονία with the help of several key phrases, and these phrases should receive prominence in research on εὐδαιμονία in *EN*. These phrases found at the major signposts from I.7 and X.6 need to be explored further.

In this chapter, I present an argument about how Aristotle intended his readers to read his inquiry on εὐδαιμονία in *EN*. A wise reading of Aristotle's text will seek to follow his signposts. This is what I will try to do in the first section of this chapter: I will show where these signposts are and examine their meaning. I will argue that the first one in *EN* I.7 is best interpreted as speaking about the action of delineating a perimeter. The second signpost from *EN* X.6 is best interpreted as meaning the action of leaving an imprint on an object.

Then, in the second section, focusing on the term εὐδαιμονία, Aristotle tells the reader that although everyone agrees that this is the right word for describing the ultimate end of man, there is no agreement as to its meaning. Aristotle gives the reader several options proposed by others, and then evaluates and dismisses them. The contemporary reader needs to understand as clearly as possible what others in the ancient Greek world have said about εὐδαιμονία, and then, based on those insights, s/he will have a better understanding of what Aristotle proposes in his inquiry in *EN*. That is why the second section of this chapter is about pre-Aristotelian literature on εὐδαιμονία. I will study the main affirmations made by the Greek authors beginning with Sapho and ending with Lycurgus. I will argue that Aristotle is the first Greek author to provide the most systematic teleological understanding of happiness based on two metaphors: "perimeter of the good," and the "imprint of happiness."

3.2 READING THE ARGUMENT ON HAPPINESS IN *EN* THROUGH ITS MAIN SIGNPOSTS

In his inquiry about εὐδαιμονία Aristotle employs two main criteria: finality and function. This is done in *EN* I.1–7. At the end of this major section, in *EN* I.7 1098a21–24, there is the first important signpost. And at the end of the whole inquiry, in *EN* X.6 1176a30–32, is the last signpost that says what was done in the whole inquiry. These two signposts offer essential summaries and hermeneutical keys for how to read the whole study. Thus, in this section I will study these two important texts by focusing on the critical terms "perimeter" and "imprint." I will argue that these phrases give readers the key to understand Aristotle's inquiry as the process through which a form is shaped within a clearly defined perimeter.

Here it is the first major signpost in *EN*:

> Let this account then serve to describe the Good in outline [περιγεγράφθω τἀγαθὸν]—for no doubt the proper procedure is to begin by making a rough sketch, and to fill it in afterwards. If a work has been well laid down in outline [τῇ περιγραφῇ], to carry it on and complete it in detail may be supposed to be within the capacity of anybody. (*EN* I.7 1098a21–24)[1]

> Having now discussed the various kinds of Virtue, of Friendship and of Pleasure, it remains for us to treat in outline of Happiness [εὐδαιμονίας τύπῳ], inasmuch as we count this to be the End of

1. Rackham, *Nicomachean Ethics*.

human life. But it will shorten the discussion if we recapitulate what has been said already. (*EN* X.6 1176a30–32)[2]

I gave the Greek terms in square brackets to show something essential about the way the reader has to understand what Aristotle does in his study. These two main signposts use two different terms to describe what Aristotle does in his inquiry: the first one [περιγράφω]which is part of the phrase translated as "the Good in outline" [περιγεγράφθω τἀγαθὸν], and the second [τύπος] which is part of the phrase "outline of Happiness" [εὐδαιμονίας τύπῳ]. Other scholars translate the phrase περιγεγράφθω τἀγαθὸν as: "an outline of the good,"[3] or "the good have been sketched in this way,"[4] or "let the good, then, be sketched in this way,"[5] or "a sketch of the good."[6] Other scholars translate the phrase εὐδαιμονίας τύπῳ as: "in outline the nature of happiness,"[7] or "an outline account of happiness,"[8] or "in outline what concerns happiness,"[9] or "happiness by giving an outline of it,"[10] or "outline the nature of happiness,"[11] or "happiness in outline."[12]

Aristotle's project starts with a section that is described with the help of περιγράφω, and its outcome is described with the help of τύπος. When the translators translate both terms with "outline" (of a book or an argument), I argue below that they miss something essential of what Aristotle actually says.

3.2.1 The perimeter of the good

Aristotle uses περιγράφω in the first major signpost of *EN* I.7 1098a21–24. This word means I. draw a line round, 2. define, determine, limit, 3. terminate, conclude, 4. bring to an end, cure a disease, II. draw in outline,

2. Rackham, *Nicomachean Ethics*.
3. Barnes, *Complete Works of Aristotle*.
4. Bartlett and Collins, *Nicomachean Ethics*.
5. Reeve, *Nicomachean Ethics*.
6. Irwin, *Nicomachean Ethics*.
7. Barnes, *Complete Works of Aristotle*.
8. Crisp, *Nicomachean Ethics*.
9. Bartlett, and Collins, *Nicomachean Ethics*.
10. Reeve, *Nicomachean Ethics*.
11. Ross, *Nicomachean Ethics*.
12. Irwin, *Nicomachean Ethics*.

trace or sketch, delineate, III. enclose as it were within brackets, cancel, annul, 2. reject as spurious, IV. defraud.[13] We need to study this term both diachronically[14] and synchronically[15] to understand as much as possible about it. Thus, I will present, in historical order, the Greek texts in which περιγράφω is used in the centuries before Aristotle, and then, in the century of Aristotle. I will argue that the action of "drawing a line around" is used as a metaphor by Aristotle to describe the delineation of a perimeter of the good in *EN*.

The earliest occurrence in the surviving Greek texts we have is from sixth century BCE in Aeschylus's *Orestia Trilogy*, ch. 207 (*Libation Bearers*). In the dialogue, between Orestes and his sister Electra, she says:

> And look! Another proof!
>
> Footprints matching each other—and like my own!
>
> Yes, here are the outlines of two sets of feet [περιγραφὰ ποδοῖν), his own and some companion's.
>
> The heels and the imprints of the tendons agree in proportion with my own tracks.[16]

In this text the contours of the imprint of someone's feet is depicted by περιγράφω, and this "contour of an imprint" is the basic idea conveyed by our term. E. D. A. Morshead translates the occurrence in this text with "footmark."[17]

In the fifth and fourth century[18] BCE philosophical political texts περιγράφω is used exactly as in our political ethical text of *EN*. I argue that Aristotle uses this term as his master, Plato, uses it in the *Laws*. Aristotle tells us in *EN* I.7 1098a21 that he needs first to "delineate a perimeter of the good," and then, later this will be "filled in." Plato in *Laws* 770b8 says something similar:

13. Liddell, Scott, Jones, and Mckenzie, *A Greek-English Lexicon*, 1371.

14. I will present a study of how περιγράφω was used in the centuries before Aristotle. The texts in which περιγράφω is used will be studied in historical order.

15. I will present a study of how περιγράφω was used in the fourth century by the authors contemporary with Aristotle, and by Aristotle himself.

16. Smyth, *Aeschylus*.

17. Morshead, *Choephori*.

18. In the fifth century BCE περιγράφω also occurs in Isocrates, *Frag* 10.16; Herodotus, *Hist.* 8.137.25; Aristophanes, *Pax* 879; Demonicus, *Fragmentum Ach.* 1.3; Hippocrates, *De decente habitu* 2.8; Empedocles, *Testimonia* 50.4; Leucippus, *Testimonia* 24.29; Oenopides, *Testimonia* 10.8 (cf. *TLG Workplace* 7.0).

Clinias

We should,—if, that is to say, we are capable of so doing.

Athenian

At any rate we must try and try hard.

Clinias

By all means.

Athenian

Let us address them thus:—"Beloved Keepers of the Laws, in many departments of our legislation we shall leave out a vast number of matters (for we need must do so); yet, notwithstanding, all important matters, as well as the general description, we shall include, so far as we can, in our outline sketch [περιγραφῇ]. Your help will be required to fill in this outline; and you must listen to what I say about the aim you should have before you in doing so.[19]

Plato makes similar points in *Laws* 768c5 ("this outline sketch serves to describe them in part"), and in 876e1 ("we stated an outline and typical cases of punishments"; [τὸ περιγραφὴν το καὶ τοὺς τύπους]). Plato's *Laws* 876e1 is particularly important for my project because it uses, in a political philosophical text, both περιγράφω and τύπος together: one with the meaning of "outline/perimeter" and the other with "types" of various punishments.

In the fourth century BCE Theophrastus and Aristotle are the main authors[20] who use our term. In *Enquiry into Plants* 9.8.8, Theophrastus uses περιγράφω in a literal way several times explaining different practices:

And many similar notions are mentioned. Thus, it is said that one should draw three circles round a mandrake with a sword [περιγράφειν δὲ καὶ τὸν μανδραγόραν εἰς τρὶς ξίφει] and cut it with one's face towards the west; and at the cutting of the second piece one should dance round the plant and say as many things as possible about the mysteries of love. (This seems to be like the direction given about cummin, that one should utter curses at the

19. Bury, *Plato*.

20. The only ancient Greek author who uses the exact form of the verb (περιγεγραφθω) is Eudemus, the famous student of Aristotle in *Fragmenta* 140.149, 140.125, 140.164. Other authors, in the fourth century BCE, who use occasionally περιγράφω are Aristoxenus, *Elementa harmonica* 9.1, Epicurus, 011 84.5, 011.88.9, Theopompus, *Fragmenta* 2b, 115, F.391.2, Hecataeus, *Fragmenta* 3a, 264, F.25.1512 (cf. *TLG Workplace 7.0*).

time of sowing.) One should also, it is said, draw a circle round [περιγράφειν] the black hellebore and cut it standing towards the east and saying prayers, and one should look out for an eagle both on the right and on the left.[21]

This text from Theophrastus, the student of Aristotle, is essential for how the term was used in the fourth century: the literal meaning of "drawing a circle round" an object was known and used in various situations.

Περιγράφω appears several times in the Aristotelian corpus (*Nicomachean Ethics* 1098a; *Gait of Animals* 743b; *Politics* 1276a; *Rhetoric* 1396b; and *Topics* 101a).[22] The occurrence in *Politics* 1276a25 is a good example of the literal meaning of the term. There Aristotle says:

> Suppose a set of men inhabit the same place, in what circumstances are we to consider their city to be a single city? Its unity clearly does not depend on the walls, for it would be possible to throw a single wall round the Peloponnesus; and a case in point perhaps is Babylon, and any other city that has the circuit [περιγραφὴν] of a nation rather than of a city.[23]

The line of the walls around a city is described by using περιγράφω.

The example from *On the Gait of Animals* 743b describes the "undulating" movement of limbless animals:

> Of limbless animals, some progress by undulations (and this happens in two ways, either they undulate on the ground, like snakes, or up and down, like caterpillars), and undulation is a flexion; others by a telescopic action, like what are called earthworms and leeches. These go forward, first one part leading and then drawing the whole of the rest of the body up to this, and so they change from place to place. It is plain too that if the two curves were not greater than the one line which subtends them undulating [ταῖς περιγραφαῖς] animals could not move themselves; when the flexure is extended they would not have moved forward at all if the flexure or arc were equal to the chord subtended; as it is, it reaches further when it is straightened out, and then this part stays still and it draws up what is left behind.[24]

---

21. Hort, *Enquiry Into Plants*.
22. *TLG Workplace 7.0.*
23. Rackhman, *Politics*.
24. Farquharson, *On the Gait of Animals*.

This image of "drawing a line round" is applied in a figurative way to delineate space, or things from other entities; the occurrence from *Rhetoric* 1396b11 is suggestive:

> As for those to be used in sudden emergencies, the same method of inquiry must be adopted; we must look, not at what is indefinite but at what is inherent in the subject treated in the speech, marking off [περιγράφοντα] as many facts as possible, particularly those intimately connected with the subject.[25]

These examples from Aristotle shows that he knows and uses περιγράφω both literally and figuratively. If I translate literally what Aristotle says in *EN* I.7 1098a21–24, I see that he uses a metaphor: he describes his political ethical inquiry in terms of "drawing a line round, delineating" the good of man. He speaks exactly as his master, Plato, does in *Laws* 770b8: first an "outline sketch," which will be filled in later. When I picture the image conveyed by his lexical choice, then, what he does in *EN* I.1–7 is "drawing a perimeter of the good of man."

Aristotle worked with two main concepts to delineate this perimeter: the ultimate end [τέλος] (*EN* I.1–7 1094a1–1097b20), and the function of man [ἔργον ἄντθρωπου] (*EN* I.7 1097b21–1098a20). He delineates with them the perimeter of the good indicating how far we can go when we inquire about it. To translate περιγράφω in *EN* I.7 1097b21 with "outline" and to understand by it "a summary of something" is to point in an unclear direction because Aristotle has written 4,081 words so far in *EN* (in the English translation), and it is a stretch to call so much text an "outline/summary."

As it can be seen by the way other scholars translate περιγράφω with "sketch"[26] we have to look somewhere else. They point us to drawing. But this is unclear too, because Aristotle does not draw as such, he is studying εὐδαιμονία. That is why I argue that here he uses a metaphor and it is the responsibility of the interpreter to explain the point of comparison as well as s/he can. "Drawing a line round something" is for the purpose of "defining" εὐδαιμονία.

The action of "marking off" as many facts as possible is communicated with the help of our term [περιγράφω]. A perimeter of meaning is established by this "drawing a line round." This is what Aristotle does in

---

25. Freese, *Art of Rhetoric*.
26. Irwin, *Nicomachean Ethics*; Reeve, *Nicomachean Ethics*.

EN concerning the meaning of the good of man. As far as I am aware, in Aristotelian studies on the good of man in *EN*, this observation has not been made yet. In the earliest ancient Greek commentary of Aspasius on *Nicomachean Ethics* there is the following comment on our text:

> Just as painters first make a rough outline, and then fill each part exactly, so too Aristotle says that the definition of happiness has first been outlined—using the term metaphorically—and then announces that he will later render it more exact.[27]

But in what follows Aspasius does not explore and does not explain the metaphor used by Aristotle. I say that what we have from Aristotle is not an "outline/summary" of the good of man, but a "perimeter" within which he makes observations and reaches varied conclusions about his subject matter. Everything inside that "perimeter" is valid information about the good of man. He will delineate this perimeter with the help of the ultimate end [τέλος] and of the function of man [ἔργον ἀνθρώπου]. In other words, he "draws the round line [of the walls]" within which the good of man is to be explored. This metaphor has political connotations.

3.2.2 The τύπος of happiness

In this section I offer a diachronic and synchronic study on τύπος in ancient Greek literature. We will consider, in historical order, the Greek texts in the centuries before Aristotle, and then in the century of Aristotle. I will focus mainly on the occurrences of τύπος in ethical contexts.

Τύπος is from *EN* X.6 1176a31, and is usually translated in *EN* with "outline." It means I. blow, II. the effect of a blow or of pressure, III. cast or replica made in a mold, IV. figure worked in relief, V. carved figure, image, VI. form, shape, VII. archetype, pattern, model, VIII. general impression, vague indication, outline, sketch, general idea, IX. prescribed form, model to be imitated, X. summons.[28] Bauer gives the following meanings for τύπος: 1. a mark made as the result of a blow or pressure, *mark, trace*, 2. embodiment of characteristics or function of a model, *copy, image*, 3. an object formed to resemble some entity, *image, statue*, 4. a kind, class, or thing that suggests a model or pattern, *form, figure, pattern*, 5. the content of a document, *text, content*, 6. an archetype serving as a model, *type*,

27. Aspasius. *Nicomachean Ethics 1–4, 7–8*, 20.
28. Liddell, Scott, Jones, and Mckenzie, *A Greek-English Lexicon*, 1835.

pattern, model.[29] These possibilities of meaning have to be assessed with reference to the context. In order to do that I need to study how τύπος is used mainly in ethical contexts, both diachronically and synchronically in the surviving ancient Greek literature.

The earliest occurrences of τύπος, in the Greek classical texts we have, are in Homer's *Iliad* and *Odyssey* (eighth century BCE). In *Iliad* 19.363, in a scene of war, Homer conveys the situation in which the blow of a loud and prolonged noise is described:

> As when thick and fast the snowflakes flutter down from Zeus chill beneath the blast of the North Wind, born in the bright heaven; even so then thick and fast from the ships were borne the helms, bright-gleaming, [360] and the bossed shields, the corselets with massive plates, and the ashen spears. And the gleam thereof went up to heaven, and all the earth round about laughed by reason of the flashing of bronze; and there went up a din from beneath the feet of men [ὑπὸ δὲ κτύπος ὄρνυτο ποσσὶν ἀνδρῶν]; and in their midst goodly Achilles arrayed him for battle.[30]

And in *Odyssey* 16.6, the sound of the return of Telemachus falls upon Odysseus's ears:

> And goodly Odysseus noted the fawning of the hounds, and the sound of footsteps fell upon his ears [περί τε κτύπος ἦλδε ποδοῖιν]; and straightway he spoke to Eumaeus winged words: "Eumaeus, surely some comrade of thine will be coming, or at least some one thou knowest, for the hounds do not bark, but fawn about him, and I hear the sound of footsteps."[31]

The same meaning of "blow" of a sound is found in the *Homeric Hymns*, Ap 262:

> The trampling of swift horses and the sound of mules [κτύπος ἵππων ὠκειάων] watering at my sacred springs will always irk you, and men will like better to gaze at the well-made chariots and stamping, swift-footed horses than at your great temple and the many treasures that are within.[32]

---

29. Bauer, *A Greek-English Lexicon*, 830.
30. Murray, *The Iliad*.
31. Murray, *The Odyssey*.
32. Evelyn-White, *The Homeric Hymns and Homerica*.

In the seventh century BCE, τύπος is used by Tyrtaeus in *Fragmenta* 19.14, which is incomplete, and in the sixth century by Aeschylus in *The Seven against Thebes*, 83: "A signal, though speechless, of doom, a herald clearer than a cry! Hoof-trampled, the land of my love bears onward the din to mine ears [ὁπλῶν κτύπος]."[33] Τύπος seems to have the same meaning of "blow" as in the eighth century BCE.

In the fifth and fourth century BCE, in political ethical contexts, Plato's usage of τύπος is most helpful. In my view, the text from *The Republic* 2.377 is the most relevant for understanding Aristotle's political usage of τύπος in the fourth century. The formation of the guardians of the state is described with the help of τύπος. This is an extensive quote of what Plato writes in *Republic* 2.376b–377a:

> SOCRATES: Philosophy, then, and spirit, speed, and strength as well, must all be combined in the nature of anyone who is going to be a really fine and good guardian of our city.
>
> GLAUCON: Absolutely.
>
> SOCRATES: Then that is what he would have to be like at the outset. But how are we to bring these people up and educate them? Will inquiring into that topic bring us any closer to the goal of our inquiry, which is to discover the origins of justice and injustice in a city? We want our account to be adequate, but we do not want it to be any longer than necessary.
>
> And Glaucon's brother replied:
>
> I for one certainly expect that this inquiry will help us.
>
> SOCRATES: By Zeus, in that case, my dear Adeimantus, we must not abandon it, even if it turns out to be a somewhat lengthy affair.
>
> ADEIMANTUS: No, we must not.
>
> SOCRATES: Come on, then, and like people in a fable telling stories at their leisure, let's in our discussion educate these men.
>
> ADEIMANTUS: Yes, let's.
>
> SOCRATES: What, then, will the education be? Or is it difficult to find a better one than the one that has been discovered over a long period of time—physical training for bodies and musical training for the soul?

33. Smyth, *Aeschylus*.

ADEIMANTUS: Yes, it is.

SOCRATES: Now, won't we start musical training before physical training?

ADEIMANTUS: Of course.

SOCRATES: And you include stories under musical training, don't you?

ADEIMANTUS: I do.

SOCRATES: But aren't there two kinds of stories, one true and the other false?

ADEIMANTUS: Yes.

SOCRATES: And education must make use of both, but first of the false ones?

ADEIMANTUS: I do not understand what you mean.

SOCRATES: Don't you understand that we first begin by telling stories to children? And surely, they are false on the whole, though they have some truth in them. And we use stories on children before physical training.

ADEIMANTUS: That's true.

SOCRATES: That, then, is what I meant by saying that musical training should be taken up before physical training.

ADEIMANTUS: And you were right.

SOCRATES: Now, you know, don't you, that the beginning of any job is the most important part, especially when we are dealing with anything young and tender? For that is when it is especially malleable and best takes on whatever pattern [τύπος] one wishes to impress on it.

ADEIMANTUS: Precisely so.[34]

This extensive quote shows how Plato understood the formation of the most important people in the city, the guardians of the state. The two areas of their education, poetry and physical training, are to be implemented in their lives from an early age. That educational process will have an impact on their development. And this impact/impression is described

34. Reeve, *Republic*.

by τύπος: "the pattern one wishes to impress on it." Other scholars translate this important text as follows: "For it is then that it is best moulded and takes the impression (τύπος) that one wishes to stamp upon it";[35] "That is the time when each individual thing can be most easily molded and receive whatever mark you want to impress upon in."[36]

I argue that Aristotle's political ethical usage of τύπος has to be understood in similar terms. In *EN* X.6 1176a31, this is an affirmation at the end of a long inquiry (Aristotle has at this point written ten books of the *EN*). So "vague indication" or "sketch" or "outline" is not the meaning of τύπος here, keeping in view the *vast* amount of work just done. I therefore, conclude that in *EN* X.6 1176a31 εὐδαιμονίας τύπῳ should be read as a metaphor: a visible impression made as the result of a blow, an "imprint of happiness." The effect of a blow that leads to a mark is what makes me translate εὐδαιμονίας τύπῳ as "imprint of happiness."

A metaphor, according to Aristotle, is "the application of an alien name by transference" (*Poetics* 3.21).[37] Aristotle "transfers" the alien name of "the mark of the blow" to an unexpected context, which is that of εὐδαιμονία. A good metaphor is "the mark of genius, for to make good metaphors implies an eye for resemblances" (*Poetics* 3.21).[38] As a result of the blow, something is formed, an imprint, and it is this the resemblance Aristotle observes between τύπος and εὐδαιμονία: the general notion of form.

Thus, based on the above study about τύπος, I go against almost all translations of *EN* into English and propose "imprint" as the meaning for τύπος in *EN* X.6 1176a31. And because Aristotle intends that this inquiry to be put in practice, based on the meaning of "imprint," I think that Aristotle intended it to become "a type" of happiness, that is, how a particular understanding of happiness is to be embraced and practiced. The argument for "outline" is weak because in *EN* I–X Aristotle provided the reader with a full inquiry into εὐδαιμονία, not just several observations as in an "outline/summary." By understanding εὐδαιμονίας τύπῳ as a metaphor meaning "imprint of happiness" I say, with Aristotle, that "ordinary words convey only what we know already, [but] it is from metaphor that we can best get hold of something fresh" (*Rhetoric* 3.10)[39] and this "something fresh" is the

35. Shorey, *Republic*.

36. Ferrari, and Griffith, *Republic*.

37. Fyfe, *Poetics*.

38. Fyfe, *Poetics*.

39. Freese, *Art of Rhetoric*.

breakthrough that is possible only with the help of a good metaphor. A good metaphor "gives style clearness, charm, and distinction as nothing else can" (*Rhetoric* 3.2).[40]

This does not mean that there are no occurrences of τύπος in *EN* where it has the meaning of "outline, sketch." In *EN* I.11 1101a28 Aristotle says: "perhaps a general outline (τύπῳ) will be enough of an answer." In *EN* I.11 Aristotle discusses in passing the happiness of the dead, and a short, sketchy discussion of the subject is enough. Another example is in *EN* II.7 1107b14: "At the moment we are speaking in outline [τύπῳ] and summary [κεφαλαίῳ], and that is enough; later we shall define these things more exactly."

The last occurrence of τύπος in *EN* is in X.9 1179a35, where Aristotle says: "If then we have sufficiently discussed in their outlines the subjects of Happiness and of Virtue in its various forms." This standard translation by Rackham shows that "outlines" is not enough to capture the meaning of what Aristotle says. The translation adds "in its various forms" to capture the meaning of τοῖς τύποις. For one word in Greek, we have several in English: "outlines . . . in its various forms," and I argue, based on my above analysis of τύπος, that Rackham is right to try to break new ground beyond what others have done and translate it as he did. By translating εὐδαιμονίας τύπῳ as "imprint of happiness" in *EN* X.6 1176a31, I believe I can point, right from the beginning, the whole analysis of my inquiry into what actually is: how εὐδαιμονία is "formed" in people's lives. This is language that has to be read into the general metaphysical framework of Aristotle, which centrally concerns movement from matter to form, from potentiality to actuality. A good reading of Aristotle's inquiry of εὐδαιμονία needs this overall metaphysical teleological framework of thought in view at all times. I will present the details of this framework of thought in 4.1.

In *EN* X.6 1176a31, there is the end of Aristotle's inquiry which starts by focusing on the unity of his inquiry. By focusing on the unity of his endeavor, he gives the reader a recapitulation of what he had said so far, and this is described by him as an εὐδαιμονίας τύπῳ ("type/imprint of happiness" *EN* X.6 1176a31). This recapitulation shows the major features of the "imprint of happiness." It is metaphysical language that reviews the stage of his inquiry in the overall movement from potentiality to actuality, or from matter to form. In this case, in the perimeter of teleology and function, I identify his findings as being expressed in metaphysical language with a

40. Freese, *Art of Rhetoric*.

variety of features. Aristotle mentions that εὐδαιμονία, as the aim of human life, has to be classed as "some form of activity" [ἐνέργειαν τινα] (*EN* X.6 1176b1), and it is to be seen among the "activities desirable in themselves" [τῶν καθ" αὑτὰς αἱρετῶν] (*EN* X.6 1176b5) because it "lacks nothing, and is self-sufficient" [ἐνδεὴς . . . ἀλλ" αὐτάρχης] (*EN* X.6 1176b6). An activity desirable in itself is an activity that does not "aim at any result beyond the mere exercise of the activity" (*EN* X.6 1176b8); noble and virtuous activities are things "desirable for [their] own sake" (*EN* X.6 1176b9). Εὐδαιμονία consists in "activities in accordance with virtue" [ταῖς κατ' ἀρετὴν ἐνεργείαις] (*EN* X.6 1177a11). At the end of this last part of his inquiry Aristotle will confirm that his overall endeavor was a discussion of "the subjects of Happiness and of Virtue in its various forms" (*EN* X.9 1179a35). This is the end of Aristotle's study intended to leave an "imprint of happiness" in people's lives. The "imprint of happiness" is thus an educational metaphor.

Thus, I argue that this is how his ethics is presented and applied: εὐδαιμονία is explained within the perimeter of teleology and function as these reach completions in the imprint of the "activity according to the highest virtue" (*EN* X.7 1177a13). Aristotle will continue and say that even when "the imprint of happiness" is presented, the endeavor is not complete because "to know what virtue is, is not enough; we must endeavor to possess and to practice it, or in some other manner actually ourselves to become good" (*EN* X.9 1179b2).

3.2.3 Conclusion

So, in this project I use these two metaphors of "perimeter" and "imprint" to guide the interpretation of εὐδαιμονία in *EN*. The first metaphor of "perimeter of the good" [περιγεγράφθω τἀγαθὸν] (*EN* I.7 1098a21) is intended to delineate what the good of man is. I argue that Aristotle does that with the help of the criteria of finality and function. The ultimate end and function of humans are the factors that "mark off" the good of man, εὐδαιμονία. This action of "drawing a line round something" is what is needed for a "more explicit account of" happiness (*EN* I.7 1097b24). The criterion of finality of εὐδαιμονία says that happiness is something "final and self-sufficient, the end at which all actions aim" (*EN* I.7 1097b20). The criterion of the function of man through which we can get a "more explicit account" of the good of man, εὐδαιμονία, is identified as being the "activity of the soul in accordance with excellence" (*EN* I.7 1098a17). This is how the "perimeter" of the εὐδαιμονία is delineated with the help of τέλος and ἔργον ἀνθρώπου.

The second metaphor of "imprint of happiness" [εὐδαιμονίας τύπῳ] (*EN* X.6 1176a31) is intended to capture the completion of the whole process of "forming" of εὐδαιμονία, which is the "activity according with the highest virtue" (*EN* X.7 1177a12). In this, the criteria of finality and function reach their climax. Finality of happiness reaches its completion into the "complete happiness" [ἡ τελεία εὐδαιμονία] (*EN* X.7 1177a17); this is teleology reaching its final aim. The criterion of function reaches its completion when the "highest virtue," the virtue of "highest thing in us" which is our intellect [νοῦς] (*EN* X.7 1177a22) guides all our activities. This is the activity of contemplation [θεωρία] (*EN* X.7 1177a19).

Aristotle's whole inquiry was intended to leave an imprint, to form a pattern of εὐδαιμονία that is known and practiced. I will argue that Aristotle's overall inquiry is intended to establish a "type of εὐδαιμονία" (*EN* 10.9 1179a35) for people to practice in their life in the city. The entire inquiry has a "ring" composition: it starts (*EN* I.2 1094a25) and ends (*EN* X.9 1179a35) by making references to "imprint"/τύπος of "the Supreme Good" (*EN* I.2 1094a25) and of "Happiness" (*EN* X.9 1179a35). Aristotle explores, within this overall "ring," εὐδαιμονία in accordance with the criteria of teleology (τέλος) and function (ἔργον ἀνθρώπου). Through this two criteria Aristotle establishes the "perimeter of the good" (*EN* I.7 1098a21). All his affirmations and inquiries on εὐδαιμονία in *EN* are done within this perimeter. Within this "perimeter of the good" Aristotle explores εὐδαιμονία further by studying "the activity of the highest virtue" which is the "virtue of the best thing in us;" this activity is the activity of θεωρία (*EN* X.7 1177a18). This is how he establishes an "imprint of happiness" (*EN* X.9 1179a35) that has to be carried out and practiced in the city.

These two metaphors of "perimeter" and "imprint" need further clarification by studying the term εὐδαιμονία itself as this is used in the surviving Greek literature before Aristotle. Aristotle himself in *EN* makes references to others before him in relation to εὐδαιμονία, and the next section is intended to enlarge the inquiry by providing the major ideas and perspectives on εὐδαιμονία before Aristotle, and in his own time in the fourth century BCE.

3.3 FROM SAPPHO TO LYCURGUS: PREARISTOTELIAN LITERATURE ON ΕΥΔΑΙΜΟΝΙΑ

This section offers an overview of how εὐδαιμονία was used in the surviving ancient Greek literature before Aristotle. I will present the data in historical order starting with the earliest author, Sappho, and going all the way to the last before Aristotle, Lycurgus. I include this section because Aristotle in *EN* I.4 1095a20–30 refers to various ways in which people explain the meaning of εὐδαιμονία. The more details we have about these ancient Greek understandings, the better our understanding of εὐδαιμονία in *EN* can become. We need to see as clearly as possible how Aristotle positions himself among other thinkers of his times.

The earliest occurrence of εὐδαιμονία in the surviving Greek literature is in the seventh century BCE, in Sappho, *Fragments* 148.2:

> Wealth without virtue is no harmless neighbor, but a mixture of both attains the height of happiness [δ" ἀμφοτέρων κρᾶσις εὐδαιμονίας ἔχει τὸ ἄκρον].[41]

Sappho sees happiness as a "height" [ἄκρον] that is attained by a mixture [κρᾶσις] of wealth and virtue. The reference to "height" is, most likely understood as language of pleasure. Although this is the only time that Sappho uses εὐδαιμονία, I interpret this saying as being part of her love for music and poetry. We know from Strabo, (*Geography* 13.2.3) that Sappho was "a marvellous woman" with no rival "in the matter of poetry."[42] It can be seen that from a very early time the Greeks understood the complexities of εὐδαιμονία and tried to find ways of conveying it in words. It has to do with virtue and wealth. As this text is a fragment of poetry there is no sufficient text or argument to put together a larger and deeper picture of Sappho's understanding of εὐδαιμονία, but it serves as a good historical starting point.

In the sixth century BCE, Pindar uses εὐδαιμονία several times in *Odes*. Pindar's approach is based on the perspective of fortune. He addresses Hieron in *Pythian Odes* 3.84 saying that: "Fools cannot bear their pain with grace, but noble men can, by turning the good side outwards. It is your lot to be attended by good fortune [εὐδαιμονίας]. For great destiny watches over the leader of the people."[43] Various victories, both in Isthmian

41. Carson, *If Not, Winter,* 299.

42 Jones, *Geography.*

43. Arnson Svarlien, *Odes.*

and Olympian games, are the source of great joy but these also are repaid with envy. So, Pindar says in *Pythian Odes* 7.21: "The abiding bloom of good fortune [εὐδαιμονίαν] brings with it both good and bad." And in the *Nemean Odes* 7.56, he says:

> Each of us differs in nature, for we are each allotted a different life. One man has this, others have something else; but for one man to win the prize of complete happiness [εὐδαιμονίαν] is impossible. I cannot say to whom Fate has handed this consummation as a lasting possession.[44]

Thus, for Pindar, εὐδαιμονία is mainly "good fortune" handed by Fate to various people; happiness is a matter of destiny. It refers to good circumstances that bring joy.

In the fifth century BCE, εὐδαιμονία it is used extensively. In what follows I will present the most relevant texts for my investigation. Thucydides, the historian, understands it mainly in terms of "prosperity." In *Hist.* 2.97.5.3 he says about the Scythians: "By these means the kingdom become very powerful, and in revenue and general prosperity [τῇ ἄλλη εὐδαιμονίᾳ] exceeded all the nations of Europe."[45] Isocrates understands εὐδαιμονία as a "blessing" when he speaks about traitors in *To Demonicus* 49.8: "for fortune places in their hands wealth and reputation and friends, but they, for their part, make themselves unworthy of the blessings [εὐδαιμονίας] which lie within their grasp."[46] But in *Against Sophists* 4.4, Isocrates criticizes them for not valuing virtue and happiness: "although they set so insignificant a price on the whole stock of virtue and happiness [τὴν ἀρετὴν καὶ τὴν εὐδαιμονίαν], they pretend to wisdom and assume the right to instruct the rest of the world."[47] The point of Isocrates is that the Sophists do not qualify to instruct people because they do not sufficiently value virtue and happiness. In *Busiris* 14.2, Isocrates brings together again happiness and excellence when says:

> And to so perfect a state of happiness [δ' ὑπερβολὴν εὐδαιμονίας] have the Egyptians come that with respect to the excellence [ἀρετῇ] and fertility of their land and the extent of their plains they reap the fruits of a continent, and as regards the disposition

---

44. Arnson Svarlien, *Odes*.
45. Jowett, *Thucydides*.
46. Norlin, *Isocrates*.
47. Norlin, *Isocrates*.

of their superfluous products and the importation of what they lack, the river's possibilities are such that they inhabit an island.[48]

In this text, Isocrates understands εὐδαιμονία as referring to "well-being" of Egyptians due to their prosperity (see also Isocrates references in *Panegyricus* 76.4, 103.5, 187.6; *Nicocles* 32.4). This prosperity depends on the river Nile which flows through the whole extent of the land and makes it very fertile. When Isocrates speaks about Athens and its failed policies in *On the Peace* 32.2, he gives a complex understanding of εὐδαιμονία in a political context:

> They fail to see that nothing in the world can contribute so powerfully to material gain, to good repute, to right action, in a word, to happiness [εὐδαιμονίαν], as virtue and the qualities of virtue. For it is by the good qualities which we have in our souls that we acquire also the other advantages of which we stand in need. So that those who have no care for their own state of mind are unwittingly disparaging the means of attaining at the same time to greater wisdom and to greater well-being.[49]

According to Isocrates in this text, wealth, good reputation, and right action constitute happiness. These are obtained not by failed policies of the state, but mainly by virtue. Isocrates understands "virtue" as referring to "good qualities which we have in our souls." This has to be seen as a refinement in defining εὐδαιμονία in Greek ancient literature. From now on, it will be related to the soul, because virtue is about the good qualities in the soul. Isocrates does not develop these insights, but in *Areopagiticus* 53.4 he will add some "standards by which one should judge whether people are genuinely prosperous [εὐδαιμονίαν] and not living in vulgar fashion." And these standards are: "sobriety of their government, the manner of their daily life, and the absence of want among all their citizens."[50] This is how well-being has to be measured. Isocrates supports "sane moderation" as the main practice to achieve well-being. Also, Sophocles, in *Antigone* 1347, mentions the fact that "wisdom is provided as the chief part of happiness" [φρονεῖν εὐδαιμονίας πρῶτον ὑπάρχει].[51] In this way in the fifth century

---

48. Norlin, *Isocrates.*

49. Norlin, *Isocrates.*

50. Norlin, *Isocrates.*

51. Jebb, *Antigone.*

BCE, there is an advancement towards the soul as the main item in inquiring about εὐδαιμονία.

Xenophon, in *Memorabilia* 1.6.10.2, mentions Antiphon as saying that "happiness consists in luxury and extravagance" [τὴν εὐδαιμονίαν οἰομένῳ τρυφὴν καὶ πολυτέλειαν εἶναι]. But Xenophon's belief is "to have no wants is divine; to have as few as possible comes next to the divine."[52] Xenophon will develop this point, talking to Socrates, in the direction of freedom focusing on the "middle path." The "middle path" is understood in social and political terms as referring to the path between rule and slavery, which is a path of "liberty, which is the royal road to happiness" (*Memorabilia* 2.1.11.4; see also *Cyropaedia* 7.5.79.5). For Socrates, according to Xenophon, happiness is identified with the "art of kingship" [τὴν βασιλικὴν τέχνην] (*Memorabilia* 2.1.17.4).

Plato, in *Symposium* 188.d.8 adds a new context to my inquiry on εὐδαιμονία in pre-Aristotelian literature, the context of Love. In the long "Eulogy of Love," there is a summary that says:

> Thus Love, conceived as a single whole, exerts a wide, a strong, nay, in short, a complete power: but that which is consummated for a good purpose, temperately and justly, both here on earth and in heaven above, wields the mightiest power of all and provides us with a perfect bliss [εὐδαιμονίαν]; so that we are able to consort with one another and have friendship with the gods who are above us.[53]

This change in focus, from prosperity to love, is important. For Plato, love is ascendant, like a ladder on which humans ascend from the reality of the senses towards the reality of the forms. And love of various things (people, laws, institutions, forms) is what makes this ascendancy possible. Love as a "complete power" provides humans with happiness. Plato in *Symposium* understands happiness as being related to items that are beyond this world; he positions his inquiry on happiness in a metaphysical perspective: through love humans can ascend towards the world of the forms and thus, acquire "a perfect bliss" (see *Symposium* 208.e.4). Plato in *Euthydemus* 291.b.6, like Xenophon in *Memorabilia* 2.1.17.4, presents Socrates as seeing εὐδαιμονία as the "kingly art" [τὴν βασιλικὴν τέχνην],[54] but he does not develop the insight. But there is a discussion in *Gorgias* 470.e.8, where Socrates elaborates

52. Marchant, *Xenophon*.

53. Fowler, *Plato*.

54. Lamb, *Plato*.

his understanding of εὐδαιμονία in relation to the Great King. This is what he says in his dialogue with Polus:

> Polus: What? Could you find out by meeting with him, and cannot otherwise tell, straight off, that he is happy?
>
> Socrates: No, indeed, upon my word.
>
> Polus: Then doubtless you will say, Socrates, that you do not know that even the Great King is happy.
>
> Socrates: Yes, and I shall be speaking the truth; for I do not know how he stands in point of education and justice.
>
> Polus: Why, does happiness [εὐδαιμονία] entirely consist in that?
> Socrates: Yes, by my account, Polus: for a good and honorable man or woman, I say, is happy, and an unjust and wicked one is wretched.[55]

In this text, according to Socrates, εὐδαιμονία consists in education [παιδείας] and justice [δικαιοσύνης]. Through education and justice, a human being becomes "good and honorable."

To this idea, Socrates adds in *Meno* 88.c.3 that "all the undertakings and endurances of the soul, when guided by wisdom, end in happiness," and "if virtue is something that is in the soul, and must needs be profitable, it ought to be wisdom, seeing that all the properties of the soul are in themselves neither profitable nor harmful, but are made either one or the other."[56] These insights from Aristotle's master, Plato, as thought by Socrates, provide a rich context in which Aristotle will refine his inquiry in the areas of [parts of the] soul, virtue, and [the dominion of] wisdom as I will argue later in 4.3.6.

The ancient Greek idea, that happiness consists in prosperity, both of the individual, and of the state/city, is developed further by Plato in the *Republic*. Plato says in *Republic* 4.421c5 that "as the entire city develops and is ordered well, each class is to be left, to the share of happiness that its nature comports."[57] The role of the guardians of the city is essential to accomplish this development and they themselves have to be happy. The life of the guardian is understood in "moderation and secure" terms. This is what Plato says in the *Republic* 5.466b8:

55. Lamb, *Plato*.
56. Lamb, *Plato*.
57. Lamb, *Plato*.

> If the guardian shall strive for a kind of happiness that will unmake him as a guardian and shall not be content with the way of life that is moderate and secure and, as we affirm, the best, but if some senseless and childish opinion about happiness [εὐδαιμονίας] shall beset him and impel him to use his power to appropriate everything in the city for himself, then he will find out that Hesiod was indeed wise, who said that "the half was in some sort more than the whole."[58]

In this text we see how important a citizen's conception of happiness is, especially when that individual is a guardian of the city/state. For Plato, to elucidate the meaning of happiness is a political priority in the *Republic*. The character of a guardian of the city is understood by Plato as "the character of the perfectly just man" (*Republic* 5.472.c.8); a guardian of the city is a type and a model for the people of the city. Plato says that "whatever we discern in them of happiness or the reverse would necessarily apply to ourselves" (*Republic* 5.472.c.8).[59] When Plato says in the *Republic* 9.580.b.2: "Do you declare who in your opinion is first in happiness and who second, and similarly judge the others, all five in succession, the royal, the timocratic, the oligarchic, the democratic, and the tyrannical man?" the answer is that "I rank them in respect of virtue and vice, happiness and its contrary." "The son of Ariston pronounced the best man and the most righteous to be the happiest, and he is the one who is most kingly and a king over himself."[60] The king of the city/state is to be the best and the most righteous individual, the happiest man. According to Plato, this is happiness as "the kingly art," the art of justice.

In the first part of the fourth century BCE, Demosthenes understands εὐδαιμονία mainly as "prosperity" in his *Orations* 24.10, 21.143.2, 25.33.7, 45.73.1.[61] Lycurgus also understands εὐδαιμονία as "prosperity" (*Against Leocrates* 4.1, 61.7, 127.13, 149.9).[62]

This diachronic and synchronic overview on εὐδαιμονία gives me the conceptual background available to Aristotle to further develop and inquire about εὐδαιμονία. Authors like Sappho, Isocrates, Sophocles, Xenophon, Socrates, and Plato are the main voices in Aristotle's rich social,

---

58. Shorey, *Plato*.
59. Shorey, *Plato*.
60. Shorey, *Plato*.
61. Vince, *Demosthenes*; Murray, *Demosthenes*.
62. Burtt, *Lycurgus*.

political, and philosophical context. Various perspectives on εὐδαιμονία such as "wealth and virtue" (Sappho, *Fragments* 148.2), "material gain, good repute, and right action" and "sane moderation" (Isocrates, *On the Peace* 32.2), "wisdom" (Sophocles, *Antigone* 1347), "the middle path" and "the art of kingship" (Xenophon, *Memorabilia* 2.1.11.4), and "love," "kingly art," "education and justice," "the soul guided by wisdom" (Plato, *Symposium* 188.d.8; *Euthydemus* 291.b.6; *Gorgias* 470.e.8; *Meno* 88.c.3), have a lot to say about εὐδαιμονία, but Aristotle is the first in the ancient Greek world to offer a *systematic teleological ethical inquiry* on εὐδαιμονία. The initial insights about the role of soul, virtue, wisdom, and justice will be integrated in a comprehensive and unique way by Aristotle. I cannot say that Aristotle develops the work of one of his predecessors, because none of them offered a systematic teleological treatise on εὐδαιμονία as Aristotle does, and none of them integrated it so deeply into their philosophical systems (though Plato comes close in the *Republic*).

3.4 CONCLUSION

In this chapter I argued for a new reading of εὐδαιμονία based mainly on the major signposts in *EN*, and as part of the larger Greek ancient philosophical context. The main Aristotelian phrases of "perimeter of the good," and the "imprint of happiness" from I.7 and X.6 constitutes the lenses necessary for a good reading of the inquiry about εὐδαιμονία. With the help of two criteria, finality and function, Aristotle delineates a perimeter for his inquiry, and then, within this perimeter, εὐδαιμονία is to be formed in the lives of the people of the city. For Aristotle, εὐδαιμονία is ἐνεργεία, which means that happiness is the actuality of every human being. The ultimate end and the fulfilled function of every human being constitutes the metaphysical teleological framework for understanding εὐδαιμονία in the worldview of Aristotle. This upward inquiry ends up with an analysis of the actuality of our intellect, the highest part of us. The activity of θεωρία will be the highest and the complete activity of us, humans. This will be the "complete happiness."

This proposed reading is developed by Aristotle in a very rich context. Several other important philosophers have expressed their thought on this subject. I offered a detailed overview of their positions following a diachronic and synchronic approach. The vast array of conceptions and understandings of εὐδαιμονία is given by the following main terms: wealth, virtue, good repute, right action, sane moderation, wisdom, art of kingship, love, kingly art, education, justice, the soul guided by wisdom. I argued that Aristotle is the first author to provide the most systematic teleological treatment of εὐδαιμονία in the ancient Greek literature known to us. He builds his understanding on the work of his master, Plato, and on the work of others. But his argument, based on the two main metaphors: "perimeter of the good," and "the imprint of happiness," is unique to him. For Aristotle, happiness constitutes actuality. Happiness is the ultimate end where our potentiality reaches actuality. In the next two chapters I will present the arguments for this understanding of εὐδαιμονία in *EN*.

CHAPTER 4

THE PERIMETER OF THE GOOD

4.1 INTRODUCTION

SO FAR IN THIS book, in Chapter 2, I argued that Aristotle's inquiry on εὐδαιμονία, in *EN*, is best understood if the reader follows the major signposts from I.7 1098a21 and X.6 1176a30. The known three questions (see 2.2), explored in the debates on the meaning of εὐδαιμονία are important, but the focus should be on Aristotle's own signposts when his inquiry on εὐδαιμονία is studied. In Chapter 3, I argued that these two important signposts contain two important phrases: "perimeter of the good," and the "imprint of happiness," which explain how Aristotle wants the reader to understand what he wrote. Then, I argued that the ancient Greek literature, before Aristotle, used the term εὐδαιμονία to describe a vast number of things: wealth, virtue, good repute, right action, sane moderation, wisdom, art of kingship, love, kingly art, education, justice, the soul guided by wisdom, but it is Aristotle who is first in inquiring about it by delineating a perimeter with the help of two criteria: finality and function; and within this "perimeter," happiness can be formed and practiced.

Thus, for delineating the "perimeter of the good" (*EN* I.7 1098a21) Aristotle uses two criteria: finality and function (see 3.2.1 and 3.2.2). In this chapter I will explore both of them. I will study the criterion of finality in dialogue with Richardson Lear (Chapter 4.2.1), and then, by presenting my argument for a metaphysical teleology as the right perspective to understand this criterion (Chapter 4.2.2, 4.2.3). Next, I will study the criterion of function in dialogue with Kraut (Chapter 4.3.1), Korsgaard (Chapter 4.3.4), and Annas (Chapter 4.3.5). Then, I will present my argument for a metaphysical understanding of function and actuality of the soul (Chapter 4.3.6). So, I will argue that these two criteria are metaphysical in outlook and, keeping in view that Aristotle guides all his inquiry to be an "imprint of εὐδαιμονία" (EN X.6 1176a30), this metaphysical outlook is not surprising. Ultimately Aristotle argues for a theory of becoming in his ethics.

I will show that the perimeter of his theory of the good of man, εὐδαιμονία, is teleological and metaphysical. When Aristotle "draws a line round" to delineate the good, he establishes the territory in which he will operate. The good for Aristotle in EN will be understood within the limits of this perimeter. This perimeter is delineated by two main metaphysical concepts: τέλος and ἔργον ἄνθρωπου. The first term, τέλος, is used by Aristotle to establish the overall movement and aim of his inquiry about εὐδαιμονία, and the second, ἔργον ἄνθρωπου, is used to establish what is the best of man.

4.2 ΕΥΔΑΙΜΟΝΙΑ AS ΤΕΛΟΣ

The summary provided by Aristotle in EN I.7 1097b20 says that "happiness, therefore, being found to be something final and self-sufficient, is the end at which all actions aim." This affirmation identifies the components of the first criterion of finality: the self-sufficient end is the aim of all actions. According to Aristotle, this final end is to be identified with the aim of politics (EN I.4 1095a15). In this section I will explore the aspects of teleology (Chapter 4.2.2, 4.2.3), politics (Chapter 4.2.4), and self-sufficiency (Chapter 4.2.5) of εὐδαιμονία as they are developed by Aristotle in EN I.1–7. I will argue that Aristotle's metaphysical teleology is the foundation for his teleological ethics, that εὐδαιμονία is a political concept, and accordingly, its self-sufficiency is a relational political concept. Thus, the finality of εὐδαιμονία, in EN, has to be understood in the light of metaphysics and politics.

The debated aspects in the scholarly literature on εὐδαιμονία are mainly those related to the inclusive/dominant debate. I discussed this debate in 2.3.1, but I mention it here because almost every scholar who discusses the teleological section of Aristotle's inquiry directs her/his work in such a way as to position himself/herself in one or the other camp of the debate. The most recent and detailed scholarly argument published on the finality of εὐδαιμονία is that of Richardson Lear.[1] I will present her argument, and then, I will debate her and argue for a different understanding of εὐδαιμονία as τέλος according to the thesis I mentioned above.

4.2.1 Richardson Lear on the criterion of finality

The structure of Richardson Lear's inquiry is built by exploring the general meaning of an Aristotelian *telos,* teleology in *EN*, teleology, desire, and the middle-level ends, two possible solutions to the puzzle of *EN* I.7, and a critical analysis of Ackrill's inclusivist position. Richardson Lear uses the section on the "criterion of finality" to strengthen her case that we should understand εὐδαιμονία as a "monistic end."[2] Richardson Lear's thesis is that "Aristotle's conception of *telos* in the *Nicomachean Ethics* is the same one he uses in his biological works."[3]

An Aristotelian *telos*, according to Richardson Lear, is "a result" and it says that something has been accomplished.[4] To defend this understanding of τέλος Richardson Lear gives the example from *Physics* II.2194a, where she says that the "end of change" is "its stopping point."[5] She also says that *telos* as a result and the process that leads to it should not be separated;[6] τέλος is the good a change achieves (*Phys* II.2194a).[7] For example, health is the result of walking (*Phys* II.3 194b32). Richardson Lear also mentions that Aristotle, in *Physics*, "virtually equates form and *telos*" (*Phys* II.2194a, II.8199a, II.9200a). She does not give prominence to this observation when she states her thesis on the criterion of finality. She focuses mainly on the biological aspect of *telos*. Her refined understanding of *telos* in *Physics* is as a "normative standard" (*Phys* 2.7198a),[8] something we use to evaluate how well something ends. Richardson Lear says that this understanding of *telos* in *Physics* has to be taken as a "technical concept"[9] that is also used in *EN*. In *EN*, Richardson Lear says that there is a correspondence between

1. Richardson Lear, *Happy Lives*.
2. Richardson Lear, *Happy Lives*, 10.
3. Richardson Lear, *Happy Lives*, 10.
4. Richardson Lear, *Happy Lives*, 11.
5. Richardson Lear, *Happy Lives*, 11.
6. Richardson Lear, *Happy Lives*, 11.
7. Richardson Lear, *Happy Lives*, 12.
8. Richardson Lear, *Happy Lives*, 14.
9. Richardson Lear, *Happy Lives*, 15.

the ends of humans and the ends in nature as both of these are goods that determine what is needed to succeed.[10] Also, she mentions that Aristotle observes that when ends are hierarchical the higher the ends the better,[11] and that the end of a higher activity is the end that "determines the form" of a lower, subordinate end,[12] and for how long these subordinate ends are worth pursuing.[13] According to Richardson Lear, the ultimate good, happiness, is the "convergent end," it is the "terminus of all a person's choices."[14]

The next essential move Richardson Lear makes in her inquiry is the inclusion of the "function argument" in the criterion of finality. She does this because she interprets Aristotle's understanding of ultimate end for every living being as being their function.[15] This leads to her observation that, in Aristotle, the end of something "determines its essence and form,"[16] and also that the "excellent functioning is the end."[17]

The order in the structure of Richardson Lear's inquiry concerning the criterion of finality is strange at this point, because she treats the self-sufficiency of εὐδαιμονία after the function of man argument. In *EN* the order is the other way, the function of man appearing later, in *EN* I.7 1097b21–1098a20. She understands the self-sufficiency of the human being as meaning that someone by himself can make his life desirable and have everything is needed;[18] this sufficiency is the sufficiency of the ultimate aim of the best chosen life.[19] Richardson Lear says that the criterion of self-sufficiency determines how we select and aim at our ultimate target;[20] the criterion of self-sufficiency helps us to organize the best chosen life.[21] This criterion is about the relationship between what is best, the highest good, and the satisfaction we have living a life that is geared towards it.[22]

10. Richardson Lear, *Happy Lives*, 15.

11. Richardson Lear, *Happy Lives*, 17.

12. Richardson Lear, *Happy Lives*, 17.

13. Richardson Lear, *Happy Lives*, 17.

14. Richardson Lear, *Happy Lives*, 22.

15. Richardson Lear, *Happy Lives*, 22.

16. Richardson Lear, *Happy Lives*, 22.

17. Richardson Lear, *Happy Lives*, 44.

18. Richardson Lear, *Happy Lives*, 47.

19. Richardson Lear, *Happy Lives*, 48.

20. Richardson Lear, *Happy Lives*, 51.

21. Richardson Lear, *Happy Lives*, 51.

22. Lear, *Happy Lives*, 69.

My criticism of Richardson Lear's interpretation of the criterion of finality in *EN* is focused on four main aspects: 1) The evidence provided about the meaning of τέλος in Aristotle is very limited compared with its vast usage in the Aristotelian corpus and *EN*, 2) the "function" argument is not part of the "finality" argument in *EN*, 3) the self-sufficiency of εὐδαιμονία is not developed by Aristotle as much as Richardson Lear develops it, and 4) the political aspect of the criterion of finality is missing from Richardson Lear's inquiry into its meaning.

My first objection is that Aristotle's concept of τέλος in *EN* has to be approached by first letting Aristotle speak for himself in *EN*. When we search for an Aristotelian concept of τέλος we need to be guided by the work we are studying; that book has to show us the directions to follow in constructing a background of meaning for the concept under scrutiny. Aristotle has an extensive usage of τέλος in *EN*.[23] I identify three major areas covered by his concept of τέλος: 1) the overall metaphysical perspective that "the Good is that at which all things aim" (I.1 1094a18), 2) the overall political perspective that "the Good of man must be the end of the science of politics" (I.1 1094b6), and 3) the overall virtue perspective in which the "virtue ensures the rightness of the end aimed at, [and] prudence ensures the rightness of the means we adopt to gain that end" (VI.12 1144a32). Thus, based on *EN*'s usage, the directions of metaphysics, politics, and virtues have to be the lines to investigate, expand, and deepen into the meaning of τέλος in the Aristotelian corpus. In all surviving writings of Aristotle, τέλος is used 503 times.[24] It is surprising that from this vast usage Richardson Lear works only with *Physics* 2, sections 2 and 3. She does not explain this drastic selection she makes.

My second objection is about the inclusion of the "function argument" into the criterion of finality. The structure of the *EN* I.1–7, where Aristotle expands his teleological aspect of εὐδαιμονία, does not contain the "function argument." Εὐδαιμονία as τέλος is explored in I.1 1094a1—I.7 1097b20. At the end of this long inquiry, Aristotle says: "happiness, therefore, being

---

23. *EN* 1094a.18, 1094b.6, 1095a.5, 1095b.23, 1095b.31, 1097a.21, 1097a.23, 1097b.21, 1098b.19, 1099b.17, 1099b.30, 1100a.11, 1100a.32, 1101a.18, 1110a.13, 1111b.27, 1112b.15, 1112b.34, 1113b.4, 1114b.1, 1114b.14, 1114b.16, 1114b.18, 1114b.24, 1115b.13, 1115b.20, 1115b.22, 1117b.1, 1117b.3, 1139b.2, 1139b.3, 1140a.29, 1140b.6, 1140b.7, 1141b.12, 1142b.29, 1142b.30, 1142b.31, 1142b.33, 1143a.9, 1143b.10, 1144a.32, 1145a.5, 1145a.6, 1152b.23, 1153a.9, 1153a.10, 1153a.11, 1174b.33, 1176a.31, 1176b.28, 1176b.31, 1176b.35, 1179a.34, 1179b.1 (Cf. *TLG Workplace 7.0*).

24. *TLG Workplace 7.0*.

found to be something final and self-sufficient, is the End at which all actions aim" (*EN* I.7 1097b20). After this long section, and based on its findings, Aristotle continues his inquiry by saying that "we still require a more explicit account of what constitutes happiness." In other words, εὐδαιμονία as τέλος brought us so far (something final and self-sufficient), but we need to explore more what constitutes it, and for this, says Aristotle, we need to "ascertain what is man's function" [τὸ ἔργον ἀνθρώπου] (*EN* I.7 1097b25). Thus, Aristotle's "function of man" argument is not part of the τέλος argument as Richardson Lear interprets it, but builds on it by directing our attention from the general areas of metaphysics and politics to that of anthropology. This is the reason I treat the "function of man" as a separate section in my work on εὐδαιμονία, and not as a subsection in the τέλος section.

My third objection is that the self-sufficiency of happiness is the most extended section in Richardson Lear's chapter on the criterion of finality. I believe that the reason for this is that this aspect will contribute most to strengthen her position on happiness as a monistic end. But in *EN* I, the self-sufficiency as related to the finality of εὐδαιμονία is a very short section (I.7 1097b10–20), and the main perspective upon it is political. This discrepancy of space allocated to it by Richardson Lear should make the reader suspicious. Self-sufficiency as related to εὐδαιμονία as τέλος is a necessary aspect to investigate, but within much less space and importance.

My fourth objection about Richardson Lear's argument in her "criterion of finality" is that the political aspect of τέλος is missing. The good of man is the end of the science of politics (*EN* I.2 1094b8), and, surprisingly, this aspect of "life in the πόλις" is unexplored by Richardson Lear. As I will argue later in this chapter, this aspect is a major component in Aristotle's understanding of εὐδαιμονία as τέλος.

4.2.2 A teleological outlook

Based on these four objections I will build my argument for an explanation of the meaning of εὐδαιμονία as τέλος. I will focus my inquiry on the main teleological sayings from *EN* (section 4.2.2.2), and I will propose a metaphysical framework to explain them based on *Metaphysics* XII (in the larger context of *Met* I, II, V, and IX). As there are no in-depth studies that explore Aristotelian metaphysics as the foundation of his teleological ethics, in this section I will work mainly with Aristotle. Based on Aristotle's usage of τέλος in *EN*, I am guided towards a metaphysical and socio-political background. These are the components of the teleological outlook on εὐδαιμονία which I propose in this chapter.

Thus, in the section 4.2.2.1, I will explain Aristotle's teleological outlook from *EN* I as being best interpreted in the larger metaphysical framework provided by *Metaphysics*. I will present this framework of thinking in the section 4.2.2.2. I will argue that, ultimately, in Aristotle's worldview, the unmovable substance, god, is the ultimate aim, the pure actuality for every potentiality in the universe, and that the Aristotelian ethics is ultimately founded on his metaphysics. Aristotle's teleology is metaphysical and because of this, movement and change are possible. Thus, his ethics is founded on his teleological metaphysics.

4.2.2.1 *Aiming at some good*

"Aiming at some good" [ἀγαθοῦ τινὸς ἐφίεσθαι] is the main teleological presupposition brought into the inquiry right from the beginning of the *EN* I.1. Aristotle does not say why it is that everything we do aims at some good;[25] he simply presupposes it. The selection of endeavors is art/craft [τέχνη], inquiry/method [μέθοδος], action/practical pursuit [πρᾶξις], and undertaking/choice [προαίρεσις] (*EN* I.1 1094a1). He sees all of these as "aiming at some good"[26] And then, based on this observation, he says that the good is that at which all things aim. The selection of activities (art, inquiry, action, choice) is representative for "all things" in the inquiry that follows.

This "aiming at" is spoken of by focusing on the ultimate point of it: the end [τέλος]. People do something with a good in view. This is Aristotle's first move in the inquiry; his worldview is oriented towards good. Here, in *EN* I.1 1094a1, he does not prove his point, but only states it. It can be said that there are actions that are aimed at something other than the good, such as destruction, suffering, and death, but Aristotle does not offer space for such cases. Instead, he elaborates the fact that different activities have different ends, and these particular ends have this "good" in view. For example, he says that the end of medical work is health (*EN* I.1 1094a8). A factor in Aristotle's inquiry is the intentionality of the good. For example, in the art of medicine the intended good is health, but this does not mean

25. It is a matter of debate if Aristotle committed a logical blunder at this point. For an in-depth analysis, see Kenny, "Happiness," 94–96, Broadie, *Ethics*, 8–9.

26. ἀγαθοῦ is perhaps a genitive of relation; we have here a generic substantival usage.

that it will always be accomplished. Sometimes health will not be obtained. Even if the doctor tries everything, the patient will continue to be sick or even die. But the intention to do good was there all the time. Thus, "aiming at the good" does not necessarily mean that it will always be obtained.

Thus, the orientation of Aristotle's outlook is in terms of aiming at an end. And, of special interest, is that this end is the good of every process. In Aristotle's worldview there are several causes of this process: the essential nature of a thing, the matter, the source of motion, and the good; these causes are given by him in *Metaphysics* I.983b. He speaks about the "final cause of a thing" in terms of an "end." All things happen "for its sake." This type of language is common to *Metaphysics* (see II.994b) and *EN* (see I.1 1094a1). His metaphysics and his ethics both share this teleological foundation. The "end" of everything is never a means towards something, but it is always the aim for which everything happens. The nature of this "end" is the reason for its finality. It is for the sake of this end that everything happens; the nature of the ultimate end is good in itself. This good in itself is the aim of everything in the universe.

Working with the "end" as one of the "causes" Aristotle underlies the active role of the "end." The "end" is not passive or inactive. Someone does something because s/he intends to reach an aim/a goal. Aristotle uses the example of walking as a means towards being healthy (*Met* V.1013a). The "end" and the "good" are not dependent on anything. When something reaches its "end" it reaches completeness or perfection. That stage cannot be surpassed, there is nothing beyond it. It is excellent and lacking in nothing. This activity towards an end is a process that includes the end. The end of it is in view and we can reach and experience it. Walking for being healthy comprises the end in itself and is also oriented towards it: we become healthy, and we are healthy.

Reaching the "end" has to be understood in the Aristotelian framework of thought as potentiality reaching actuality (*Met* IX.1050a). In Aristotle's world if something is generated, it moves towards a principle/an end. That "end" is its actuality. The potentiality in everything is driving that thing towards actuality. Everything that is in something potentially reaches its actuality as its aim.

The two basic elements that make up every object in the world are matter and form. The matter of every object is the stuff from which that object is made. For example, the matter of a statue is marble, or wood, or metal. The form is what was made out of that matter. For example, the form of a statue says what the marble or the wood have become. The form gives the identity of what was made out of that matter. That piece of marble, or wood has the potentiality of becoming a statue. The potentiality of matter is in attaining a form. Aristotle uses the examples of a sculptor and a teacher saying that a piece of marble becomes a statue because someone gave it a form; a teacher reaches his aim when his students perform well. The sculptor is the (immediate) mover of matter into form (*Met* V.1013a-b).

4.2.2.2 Contemplation on the immovable substance

In *Metaphysics*, Aristotle focuses his inquiry/contemplation [θεωρία] on substance[27] [οὐσία]. The reason for this "contemplation" is that the substance can offer us an understanding of the principles, elements, causes, as these belong to it; they are principles of substance, the elements of substance and the causes of substance. The common ground of Aristotle's θεωρία is found both in *Met* XII and in *EN* X. *EN* X is an example of this activity of contemplation and intellectual inquiry. In *Met* XII, he contemplates on οὐσία, and in *EN* X contemplation is depicted as τελεία εὐδαιμονία. For Aristotle, the "beholding of the mind" is the highest of activities and the tool to investigate reality (*Met* XII.1072b). In both of these texts the activity of θεωρία is focused ultimately on god (the immovable οὐσία).

His contemplation on οὐσία leads him to say that there are three kinds of substances: sensible eternal, sensible perishable, and immovable (*Met* XII.1069a). The first two, he says, are studied in physics, and the third is studied in another science (*Met* XII.1069b). In *Met* XII he focuses on the immovable οὐσία. Οὐσία does not need other things for its existence, and among all the categories, οὐσία is the only one that can exist apart (*Met* XII.1069a). That is why Aristotle views it as having primacy and as being eternal (*Met* XII.1069a). Its very essence is actuality, and it does not have matter (*Met* XII.1069b). The unmovable aspect of οὐσία is important for Aristotle because he uses it for arguing that god is perfect (*Met* XI.1064a). There is no change/movement in god, but god is the source of all change and movement. God is, for Aristotle, the "unmoved mover" (*Met* XII.1072b).

There is no movement without a cause. Things like wood do not move by themselves; a carpenter is needed (*Met* XII.1071b). These two, that which moves and that which is moved, are intermediate, which means that

27. For the most recent research on how best to translate οὐσία in Aristotle as either "substance" or "essence" or "being" see Kosman, *Virtues*, 278–79.

they are somewhere on the chain of movement, not at the beginning, nor at the end of it. For arguing about the beginning of movement Aristotle goes all the way back on the chain of movement and says that the movement starts when "there is something which moves without being moved" (*Met* XII.1072a). This is the climax of his contemplation about οὐσία: the unmoved mover is "eternal, substance, and actuality" (*Met* XII.1072a), and moves without being moved by thinking. The starting point of movement is thinking [ἀρχὴ γὰρ ἡ νόησις] (*Met* XII.1072a). Aristotle says that "the thought is moved by the object of thought" [νοῦς δὲ ὑπὸ τοῦ νοητοῦ κινεῖται], (*Met* XII.1072a).[28] The "object of thought" is the substance [οὐσία] that exists actually, and this is what moves the thought without moving.

The "actuality" aspect of the unmoved mover makes it to be the aim of every action, and every action is done for the unmoved mover's good. Aristotle goes that far that he speaks about "loving" the final cause. It does not move by being moved, but by being loved [κινεῖ δὴ ὡς ἐρώμενον] (*Met* XII.1072b); its mode of being is good.

Aristotle's conception of the unmoved mover has to be studied in more detail because it offers a better context for his conceptions about the possibility and factors of change in his universe, and it offers the metaphysical teleological foundation for his teleological ethics. In *Met* XII, Aristotle presents his argument for the unmoved mover. I will follow Easterling, Stewart and Organ's suggestions that "the distinctions made in the *Physics*, particularly Book VIII, must be applied to Aristotle's discussion of the unmoved mover in *Metaphysics* XII,"[29] and that "*Metaphysics* XII seems to combine the physical theory of *Physics* VIII with the earlier causation of *De Philosophia*."[30]

Thus, what we have in *Met* XII offers a fair representation of what Aristotle thought about the unmoved mover and its role in the universe. I will argue that in *Met* XII the Aristotelian argument for the unmoved mover is built with reference to substance and actuality, necessity and movement, contemplation and goodness. These pairing concepts need to be understood together in order to arrive to what Aristotle argues for in *Met* XII.

Aristotle's argument for the unmoved mover is part of his inquiry about οὐσία (*Met* XII.1). The relationship of the οὐσία with the universe is in terms of being the "first part" of universe (*Met* XII.1069a), pointing thus

28. Ross, *Metaphysics*.

29. Stewart, "Unmoved Mover," 522; Organ, "Unmoved Mover," 298.

30. Easterling, "Unmoved Mover," 264.

towards its principles. The principles (and causes) are three: "that by which it is changed is the *unmoved mover*; that which is changed, the *matter*; that into which it is changed, the *form*" (my italics, *Met* XII.1070a).[31] Οὐσία does not need other things for its existence; among all the categories, οὐσία is the only one that can exist apart. That is why Aristotle sees it as having primacy. Its very essence is actuality. The sensible οὐσία is changeable (*Met* XII.1069a) because "all things come out of that which is" (*Met* XII.1069b)[32] and the immovable οὐσία is eternal, "not generable but movable" (*Met* XII.1069b).

There is change and movement in the universe. Change implies the existence of an "immediate mover" (*Met* XII.1070a) and, in Aristotle's view, is a change from "matter" to "form" (*Met* XII.1070a), that is from the stuff something is made of to the particular kind of thing it is. The substances can exist apart by themselves and "all things have the same causes" (*Met* XII.1071a), meaning that without substances there is no movement and change. This change has the route from potentiality to actuality (*Met* XII.1069b). Every substance has its potentiality that has to be reached in higher forms of being towards the perfection/actuality of the unmoved mover, who is pure actuality (*Met* XII.1072b).

The movement from "substance" to "necessity" is offered by the existence of the unmovable substance. The unmovable substance is a necessity (*Met* XII.1071b). Aristotle's argument needs something capable of moving other things but not itself moving (*Met* XII.1071b).[33] Aristotle needs this because he conceives perfection in this way, if something/someone moves or changes that means it is not perfect. But god is perfect, so he does not move. He explains movement based on the necessity of an "existing cause" (*Met* XII.1071b), a mover, a cause that is already there.

Aristotle's most complete axiom is given in *Met* XII.1072a where he says that "there is something which moves without being moved, being eternal, substance, and actuality."[34] This is the climax of Aristotle's inquiry [θεωρία] about the immovable οὐσία. Aristotle explains movement "without being moved" (*Met* XII.1072a) with the help of desire and thought. He observes that when we think about something, that object is able to move our thought. This interaction between intellect and its object offers him a

31. Ross, *Metaphysics.*
32. Ross, *Metaphysics.*
33. Ross, *Metaphysics.*
34. Ross, *Metaphysics.*

way of explaining how something moves without being moved. Aristotle says that in a similar way "the final cause produces motion as being loved" (*Met* XII.1072b).[35] This abrupt introduction of "love" in his argument is to be understood in the general framework of movement from potentiality to actuality. The immovable οὐσία is pure actuality, the perfect climax, and everything else is on its way from potentiality to actuality. Because of this aspiration to actuality on the part of everything, the pure actuality, the immovable οὐσία is loved. This is how the movement of the "first kind of change" (*Met* XII.1072a) takes place. Because there is motion/change there is a first mover. This "first principle or primary being" produces the primary eternal and single movement (*Met* XII.1073a).

The relevance of this inquiry into Aristotle's metaphysics for my project is to be seen in the fact that, for Aristotle, the change from matter to form, from potentiality to actuality is possible because of the unmoved mover/god. If this external cause is not taken into account there is no change for the good, there is no reaching the ultimate end. The last pairing concepts of contemplation and goodness, in the Aristotle's inquiry on immovable οὐσία, develop the discussion in this direction.

The other angle from which Aristotle argues for the existence of the "final cause" is that of the action of the good. This angle is less developed in *Met* XII but important nonetheless, especially for my project. Its relevance is in the area of love and thinking. Aristotle says about the final cause that "its mode of being is good" (*Met* XII.1072b).[36] So far, the immovable οὐσία/the unmoved mover/god was seen as the first cause, the pure actuality, but now a different aspect is introduced, god as νοῦς/thought. Understanding god as νοῦς,[37][38] leads Aristotle deeper into the relationship between thinking and goodness. God as νοῦς shows how good is a cause of motion.[39] If the "thinking is the starting point" of every movement and change, and if god's mode of being is good, then "thinking in itself deals with that which is best in itself" (*Met* XII.1072b).[40] This thinking in itself or the "act of contemplation" [θεωρία] is a continuous state for god (*Met* XII.1072b). The most pleasant

35. Ross, *Metaphysics*.

36. Ross, *Metaphysics*.

37. Olson, "Aristotle on God," 101

38. Olson, "Aristotle on God," 101; Russell, *Philosophy*, 144; Menn, "God as Nous," 543–73.

39. Menn, "God as Nous," 573.

40. Ross, *Metaphysics*.

activity is the activity of contemplation (*Met* XII.1072b), and, based on this, Aristotle says that god "is the most good" (*Met* XII.1072b). In a way, what Aristotle himself has done so far in *Met* XII has been an intellectual activity, an inquiry [θεωρία] showing himself as an example of someone practicing it. This will reappear in my argument when I will analyze εὐδαιμονία as θεωρία later in 5.4, and Aristotle is an example of someone reaching the state of being an εὐδαίμων. Goodness is essential for Aristotle because, as the beginning is concerned, the "beauty and completeness" of being are prior to everything.

These pairs of concepts—substance/actuality, necessity/movement, and contemplation/goodness—need to be seen in their complex relationships for understanding the Aristotelian argument for the existence of the unmoved mover. The existence of the matter, and of motion, the understanding of completeness as applied to god, are the embedded layers in these various ways and angles of argumentation in Aristotle's θεωρία on immovable οὐσία in *Met* XII. These pair concepts point to the fact that his metaphysical teleology has to stay in place for his ethical teleology to work. This is the ultimate metaphysical foundation for Aristotle's teleological ethics. The criterion of finality is having the outlook that for something to be final, all actions are done for that good, and that final cause is the aim of all activities. Everything aims at the activity of intellectual inquiry, contemplation [θεωρία]; this is the telic aim of Aristotelian ethics. This activity of thinking in itself "deals with that which is best in itself" [ἡ δὲ νόησις ἡ καθ" αὑτὴν τοῦ καθ" αὑτὸ ἀρίστου] (*Met* XII.1072b).[41] In the activity of contemplation there is the convergence of "thinking" and "best" in their fullest sense, and this activity is the most pleasant and the best [ἡ θεωρία τὸ ἥδιστον καὶ ἄριστον] (*Met* XII.1072b)[42] and god is always in this good state. This overall metaphysical vision is in place when we are directed on a teleological path in ethics.

4.2.3 An end in its own right

The second move Aristotle makes in *EN* I.2 is related to our desires. Why are we doing something? The only reason Aristotle accepts for aiming at the chief good is that we are pursuing it for "its own sake." The ultimate end is not a means for something else, but for its own. In this section I will

41. Ross, *Metaphysics*.
42. Ross, *Metaphysics*.

explore this move and integrate it in Aristotle's overall vision. I will argue that an end pursued for its own sake is the final end, the convergent point, the ultimate point of an activity.

This "for its own sake" aspect of the end of our activities points away from us, toward the ultimate end, and it makes it the convergent point of everything we do. All our activities point toward this end. An aim pursued for its own sake has stability because the fragility of our humanity does not constitute the basis of our activities. Our activities are not oriented toward ourselves, but toward the supreme good [τὸ ἄριστον] (EN I.2. 1094a23). The reference to this "supreme good" is not explained clearly. Is it the good of a particular activity in the sense that it was successful or of good quality, or is it the pure actuality of this world, namely god? Perhaps it is an intended ambiguity on the part of Aristotle. In this way the reader is invited to look through the multiple layers of his or her inquiry: in the general framework of moving from potentiality to actuality, to the final cause of everything or the pure actuality that moves by being loved, the supreme good. We know how Aristotle will identify this "good:" εὐδαιμονία; a basic fact about it is that it is upward-oriented. In EN X.7 1177a13 he will define it as the "activity in accordance with the highest virtue, [. . .] of the best thing in us, which is reason, [. . .] the most divine element in us." The "upward" orientation means that it is contemplative, being oriented towards the immovable οὐσία, the god as νοῦς.

How should we understand what it is to desire something for its own sake, and not for the sake of something else? Something is desired for its own sake when it is the ultimate point of an activity, when there is nothing beyond it. The main difference is in terms of instrumentality. Something that is desired for its own sake is not an instrument to achieve something else. The other thing is that its value depends on itself not on something else; it is the final good.

By seeing the ends both as activities and products of activities (EN I.1. 1094a3) Aristotle keeps an all-encompassing view on the subject. The variety is observed, and the dynamics and completeness of ends is preserved. But not all ends are ultimate ends, some of them are subordinate or intermediate, and others are final (EN I.1 1094a2–4). The distinction between lower/subordinate/intermediate and higher/final ends corresponds to the role of different pursuits in accomplishing different ends. Some pursuits are subordinate, others are ruling, and with their ends it is the same. The higher/final ends are accomplished with the help of the lower/subordinate ends, and these higher ends of the ruling sciences/pursuits are choicer worthy than the lower ones. Their value is given by their closeness to the final activity or product of that ruling science (*EN* I.1 1094b7).

This difference between lower ends and higher ends can be analyzed from the perspective of instrumentality. According to Aristotle, if an end is chosen for its own sake it is the best good (*EN* I.2 1094a20), but if it is chosen for the sake of something else it is a lower end. An end is subordinate, intermediate, lower, if it is a means to an end that is pursued for its own sake. The focus of the observation is on the ultimate finality. Beyond that final end there is nowhere to go, there is no subordination, no intermediary. The action has arrived at its end; this end can be an activity or a product. This end is the "best good" of that action.

This understanding of the ultimate end as the best/supreme good, positions the inquiry to be an ethical inquiry. Human will and action achieve the best good. This best good cannot be transcended, that is, we cannot go beyond it. It is final and complete.

The hierarchy of actions and ends of human activities points to the science of politics as the "highest ruling science" (*EN* I.2. 1094a28). This observation positions the inquiry in the πόλις and the end or the good is going to be the good of the πόλις. So, besides the hierarchy of actions and ends, now I bring into the inquiry the life together as citizens of the city state. This makes the inquiry relevant for everyone and for all together. It is a political endeavor of the highest importance, and this is seen as the good of the city (*EN* I.2 1094b10). It is an understanding of the human good in terms of the good of the city. I will explore this in the following section.

4.2.4 The end of the science of politics

In this section I will present the scholarly context[43] in which the political aspect of Aristotle understanding of the ultimate end of humans is studied.[44] Then, I will argue that the good of the individual is understood by Aristotle as being part of the good of the state. The highest good corresponds to the

43. See Hardie, "Final Good"; Van Cleemput, "Aristotle on Happiness"; Collins, "Moral Virtue," 46–61.

44. The scholarly literature on εὐδαιμονία as the end of the science of politics is growing. I mention here the most recent works I am aware of: Donoghue-Armstrong, "Teleology," 118–66; Collins, "Moral Virtue," Arnn, "Happiness."

highest type of community, the city state. This status of being the highest type of community is given by its self-sufficiency.

The scholarly debate on εὐδαιμονία as the end of the political science in *EN* is mainly analyzed at the point of discerning what kind of end εὐδαιμονία is: inclusive or dominant (I analyzed it in 2.3.1). For example, Hardie perceives Aristotle as "fumbling" for the inclusive understanding of τέλος because the end of politics embraces other ends;[45] but in the end Hardie interprets εὐδαιμονία as a dominant end, recognizing the fact that Aristotle is ambiguous in his conception of the final good.[46]

Again, as I argued in 2.3.1, I believe that the εὐδαιμονία research has to move on beyond the inclusive/dominant debate and to explore it according to the major points and perspectives Aristotle brings/uses in his inquiry. In this case, the important question is how and why Aristotle brings politics into his inquiry? What is the common ground between *EN* and politics? This is how various scholars bring life in the city/πόλις into their interpretation of εὐδαιμονία. For Hardie, the Aristotelian definition of what is peculiar to man is the active life of the element of the soul that has a rational principle (*EN* I.7 1098a3–4) and this "action" can be understood to include contemplative thinking, as in *Politics* VII.3.[47] This is the common ground seen by Hardie between *EN* and *Politics*. This is a pioneering point, and it will be explored further by others (Van Cleemput 1999, Collins 2004). *EN* and *Politics* are part of the larger Aristotelian teleological vision, as I will show this later in this section, but Hardie does not expand on this insight and does not include *Metaphysics* and *Physics* into his interpretation of the final good.

Van Cleemput in his interpretation of εὐδαιμονία focuses his work on two major factors: man is a being that belongs in the city, and contemplation is perfect happiness.[48] These two constitute the larger framework for a political interpretation of εὐδαιμονία. According to Van Cleemput, the Aristotelian argument is not an argument that focuses primarily on the individual, but on the individual as a "political animal." That is why the Aristotelian interest is in the happiness of the πόλις.[49] Van Cleemput reaches the end of his argument by saying that in *Politics*, too, Aristotle

45. Hardie, "Final Good," 279.
46. Hardie, "Final Good," 279.
47. Hardie, "Final Good," 280.
48. Van Cleemput, "Happiness," 2, 155.
49. Van Cleemput, "Happiness," 4.

sees contemplation as happiness. The philosophical and the political lives are not separate lives, but they come together into the ideal of the mixed life. The rulers of the πόλις are those that are capable of contemplation. The perfect happiness in the city is promoted through legislation that focuses on peace and leisure.[50] Thus, these two writings *EN* and *Politics*, because both of them focus on the topic of the highest human good, they have to be interpreted together.[51]

Van Cleemput brings the political element in the interpretation of εὐδαιμονία. Aristotle says that εὐδαιμονία is the final end of the ruling science (*EN* I.2). The question is, how are these two writings, *EN* and *Politics*, related? It is likely that *Politics*, in the form we have it, is an incomplete draft.[52] That is why we do not take the work itself as something final but provisional. Thus, we have two writings (*EN* and *Politics*) from the same general science, the science of politics. Both of them have as their main theme the final end of man: εὐδαιμονία. I understand *EN* as the foundation for *Politics* not the other way around. *EN* is written with an eye on the *Politics* and informs it.

The foundational character of *EN*, as a political inquiry, is seen in its focus on the activities of the soul and transformation of character and attaining virtue. All of these are necessary for life in the city. But *Politics* can help us to unpack affirmations from *EN* where εὐδαιμονία is pictured in the larger context of the political science as it tries to ordain the life in the πόλις. The main subject of εὐδαιμονία is the final end of the political science, but in *EN* the focus is not so much on the legislation and the city work of the rulers, but on the εὐδαιμονία itself, on how should we understand it and practice it at the personal level and in relationship with others. It is more an approach from the inside out, not the vice versa. Above all things, a true student of politics has to study ἀρετή and the facts about the soul (*EN* I.13), and *EN* offers an outline for this inquiry, and *Politics* offers an integration of εὐδαιμονία in the life of the πόλις and its varied challenges.

Collins takes this relationship between *EN* and *Politics* in the understanding of the human good and explores it further. She says that, according to Aristotle, the political community and the law have an authoritative place in ordering human action.[53] For Collins, *EN* II–IV are examples of

50. Van Cleemput, "Happiness," 4.

51. Van Cleemput, "Happiness," 3.

52. Collins, "Moral Virtue," 169; Van Cleemput, "Happiness," 3; Ross, *Aristotle*, 248.

53. Collins, "Moral Virtue," 48.

how the political power orders the education and virtue of the citizens of the πόλις. She, mainly, stays within the limits of *EN* to explore the meaning of εὐδαιμονία from a political point of view. *Politics* is brought into her analysis to show how Aristotle's vision from *EN* is reflected into it. Collins does not explain the relationship between *EN* and *Politics* but shows the common ground between them in the study of political science and its final end, the good of man. The weight of the law and the final human good find an expression in terms of justice: action toward the good of another. This is our full moral perfection and the completion of virtue.[54]

Even if Collins does not focus on the meaning of εὐδαιμονία as such (her focus is on political community and virtues), she brings to our attention the necessity of working out the implications of the fact that εὐδαιμονία is the final end of the ruling political science. "Action toward the good of another" brings together both the ethical and the political. It lacks the focus on the rational element of the soul, and it does not end with θεωρία, but it points to a social understanding of the good.

In this scholarly context, the finality of εὐδαιμονία in relation to political science needs to be explored further. My project is not in Aristotle's *Politics* but because for him the good of the individual and the good of the city are the same thing, I have to explore this common ground. This common identity of εὐδαιμονία both at individual and community level is differentiated by Aristotle when he says that the good of the city is greater and more complete than the good of the individual (*EN* I.2. 1094b10).

The good of an individual and the good of the city are the same thing, but the second is greater and more complete. Aristotle does not tell us why this difference exists, but I infer from his inquiry that life in the city is seen as of greater value than the life of a single individual. Life in the city is a sign of civilization, but life alone is not. To organize a society is of greater value than to live alone. In this way, the good of the city is "greater and more complete" than the good of the individual. The difference is seen in terms of "satisfactory" and "finer and more divine" [ἀγαπητὸν/κάλλιον καὶ θειότερον] (*EN* I.2. 1094b12). This difference does not diminish the value of the individual but shows that there is something of greater value than being alone, and that is the good of the city. The reference to divinity is to be understood in the larger Aristotelian metaphysical framework. In that framework, god is the pure actuality into which every potentiality reaches its destination (see 4.2.2.2). Life in the city is closer to achieving that actuality than the

54. Collins, "Moral Virtue," 53.

life of being alone. It is us, humans, achieving a more divine good. Humans are primarily political creatures, and the good of man is to be understood as having in view the good of a nation and cities [ἔθνει καὶ πόλεσιν] (*EN* I.2 1094b10). In *Politics* I.1253a he goes that far and says that the person who does not need to live in a city is either "a beast or a god," and by this he means that, that person is self-sufficient by himself.

This relationship between πόλις and ἀγαθός is to be explored with a view at *Politics* I. In *Politics* I, Aristotle shows the details of how his political inquiry into the meaning of εὐδαιμονία works out in his political system. The premises and their conclusion at the beginning of *Politics* I.1252a are like this:

p1) humankind always acts in order to obtain that which they think good,

p2) every community is established with a view to some good,

p3) the state is the highest type of political community, and thus conclusion

c) the state aims at the highest good.[55]

In *Politics* I.1 there is the same teleological perspective as in *EN* I.1: "mankind always acts in order to obtain that which they think good." In *Politics* I, the activity of the humankind is that of establishing a πόλις, which is done with some good in view. This is true about every city. The city and the political community (*Pol.* I.1252a) is the highest type of organization and embraces all the rest, and that is why it aims at highest good. The highest good corresponds to the highest type of community, the city state.

The highest type status of the city is given by its self-sufficiency. The self-sufficiency of an entity is the result of being able to sustain itself. It depends on the ability, resources, and number. A family is more self-sufficient than an individual, and a city than a family (*Pol.* II.1261b). A city is established only when the community is large enough to be self-sufficient (*Pol.* II.1261b). Thus, based on these political insights, I will argue in the next section that the self-sufficiency of εὐδαιμονία is a relational/political concept because it depends on the self-sufficiency of the πόλις.

---

55. Jowett, *Politics*.

4.2.5 Εὐδαιμονία and self-sufficiency

In this section I will engage first with the representative scholarship about the self-sufficiency of happiness in *EN* (Ackrill, Richardson Lear, Caesar), and then, I will present my argument exploring important concepts from *EN* I and *Politics* II about self-sufficiency. I will argue that the self-sufficiency of εὐδαιμονία depends upon the self-sufficiency of the city, thus it is a political concept.

Aristotle's inquiry on εὐδαιμονία as τέλος encompasses also the aspect of "self-sufficiency." The "self-sufficiency" aspect of εὐδαιμονία is a well-researched area. Beginning with Ackrill there is the view that the self-sufficiency of εὐδαιμονία has to be understood in the larger debate about its nature as an inclusive or dominant end.[56] At this point we have another example how this debate captured the focus in εὐδαιμονία studies. As I said before, we need to move beyond it and to approach all aspects of εὐδαιμονία in their own right. And only after that should the question be raised concerning whether they play a larger role in upholding one theory or another. Ackrill argues for an inclusive understanding of εὐδαιμονία, and self-sufficiency is mainly understood in negative terms as lacking in nothing.[57] Richardson Lear, who is on the dominant side of the debate, approaches the self-sufficiency of happiness by seeing it as a "plausible constraint."[58] By this she means that when someone suffers a misfortune that person is essentially untroubled because happiness is self-sufficient; the loss of external goods does not ruin happiness. But that person will no longer have the means to be generous towards others. Happiness is sufficient by itself to make a life worth choosing. In Richardson Lear's view, this is the reason for which the self-sufficiency of εὐδαιμονία does not imply inclusiveness.[59] The ultimate good is sufficient in itself for a worthy and attractive life. The self-sufficiency of the highest good depends on its being the end of the happy life.[60]

I agree with Richardson Lear that the self-sufficiency of happiness is part of the teleological outlook of Aristotle. In *EN* I.7 self-sufficiency is a positive political concept as it is in *Politics* II.1261b. The final good is

---

56. Ackrill, "*Eudaimonia*," 65, 66.

57. Ackrill, "*Eudaimonia*," 66.

58. Richardson Lear, *Happy Lives*, 47.

59. Richardson Lear, *Happy Lives*, 48.

60. Richardson Lear, *Happy Lives*, 52.

self-sufficient because it is based on the self-sufficiency of the πόλις. The people as citizens of the political city have everything they need for a happy life. The stability of the εὐδαιμονία, when the bad events strike, is not so much based on its self-sufficiency, but on a strong character which was forged through the practice of virtues (see 4.3.6). Happiness has everything someone needs for a happy life in the sense that it is grounded in the life of the self-sufficiency of πόλις where they have protection, laws, institutions, and resources for a good life.

Because Aristotle mentions "self-sufficiency" of εὐδαιμονία without too much introduction, there are scholars who see the reference to self-sufficiency in *EN* I.7 as "an abrupt recording" that cannot be interpreted on its own.[61] Caesar reads the meaning of self-sufficiency of εὐδαιμονία in the light of *EN* X.6. Caesar understands the self-sufficiency mainly in negative terms by saying that "happines is *energeia* which is self-sufficient (lacks nothing)."[62] In my view, this is a radical and unnecessary reading because *EN* I.7 is the last major layer of Aristotle's inquiry into the finality of εὐδαιμονία. The inquiry is in the area of political science, and it is about the best life in the πόλις. The self-sufficiency is a positive concept (which can be, if necessary, expressed negatively as lacking in nothing). The city has the ability, resources and number to sustain itself. The political overview of Aristotle's inquiry has to be kept in view at all times.

I interpret Aristotle's saying about self-sufficiency of εὐδαιμονία by making reference to ideas expressed earlier in this chapter about the life in the city. Here, I start from the observation that Aristotle investigates about an end that is pursued in its own right (*EN* I.7 1097a30); it is a final end and it is for its own sake, not for the sake of something else. What does it mean "in its own right"? This phrase leads in two directions: for what it is, and for its own sake. That means that the focus is on its inherent qualities, and on the implication of having certain qualities. We are dealing with an end in itself which is not an intermediary end towards something else. It stands by itself, that is, it does not need something else. This end is pursued because of what it is in itself.

Aristotle's analysis of the "degrees of finality" [τελειότερον] (*EN* I.7 1097a30) is important because it shows the dynamics of meaning brought into inquiry by the lexical choice of τέλος. The aspects of aiming and reaching an end, and of finality go together into the mix of ideas conveyed by

61. Caesar, "Eudaimonia," 219.
62. Caesar, "Eudaimonia," 230.

Aristotle. Aristotle's argument is an "upward" one, going towards higher and higher levels. This means that it gets closer to god, the pure actuality in which all potentiality reaches its end. This is an end "more final in itself" [τέλειον τὸ καθ᾽ αὐτό] (*EN* I.7 1097a33) than any other one, it is an aim which is "absolutely final." Εὐδαιμονία is this type of τέλος because we choose it always for its own sake and not for the sake of something else (*EN* I.7 1097b2).

Based on these observations, I explore the "self-sufficiency" aspect of εὐδαιμονία. The final good is a thing "sufficient in itself" (*EN* I.7 1097b10). At this point Aristotle makes an important clarification that brings into his inquiry the political context for studying εὐδαιμονία. The self-sufficiency of the final good is not related to a life in isolation, but a life in society (*EN* I.7 1097b15). This is so because man is by nature political [φύσει πολιτικὸν ὁ ἄνθρωπος], a being who belongs to the πόλις. Self-sufficiency is a relational political concept. The highest type status of the city is given by its self-sufficiency. The self-sufficiency of an entity is the result of being able to sustain itself. It depends on the ability, resource and number. For example, a family is more self-sufficient than an individual, and a city than a family (*Pol.* II.1261b). Thus, the self-sufficiency of εὐδαιμονία is a relational/political concept because it depends on the self-sufficiency of the πόλις.

These ideas developed in *Politics* II help me to explore the text from *EN* I.7. The ultimate/complete good is self-sufficient in someone's life when this person lives in the city with his/her family, friends, and fellow citizens. Because by nature the man is political, the self-sufficiency of the ultimate good of man has to be understood in political/relational terms. The ultimate good, the self-sufficiency, and the citizenship are the lines of Aristotle's inquiry at this point.

He does not speak about the self-sufficiency of someone who lives "a solitary life" [βίον μονώτην] who is "alone/solitary by himself" [αὐτῷ μόνῳ] (*EN* I.7 1097b10). His/her existence is in the πόλις; s/he belongs in the city. The self-sufficiency of the ultimate good of people is based on the nature of man, which is a political nature. It is about life in a political community, in a city. Leaders, laws, institutions, family, friends, all are part in a political life. Self-sufficiency of happiness is based on the political nature of man. The self-sufficiency of εὐδαιμονία, the ultimate good/τέλειον ἀθαθὸν, can be attained only by living and being part in a city, because, by nature, every human is "a political thing" (*EN* I.7 1097b11).

The structure of Aristotle's inquiry has these two premises: because p1) the political community/city is more self-sufficient than a family or an individual, and

p2) man, by nature, is a political thing, it follows that conclusion

c) the self-sufficiency of the ultimate good of man is politically based.

The self-sufficiency of happiness is thus identified and, Aristotle says, it makes life desirable and lacking in nothing.

"Desirability" and "lacking in nothing" define further the self-sufficiency of εὐδαιμονία. It has everything it needs, and it is the most desired of all good things. The "lacking in nothing" of εὐδαιμονία has to be understood in the context of its self-sufficiency, that is, in its political context. A city is more self-sufficient than a solitary man. "Lacking in nothing" does not mean that εὐδαιμονία is a static activity. Its completeness is understood as aiming and reaching the ultimate goal/good. It is an upward activity that in the end likens us to the gods. I will add the references to self-sufficiency in *EN* X.6 and 8 in the chapter on θεωρία, which is the last layer in the Aristotle's upward teleological inquiry on εὐδαιμονία.

4.2.6 Conclusion

Thus, εὐδαιμονία as τέλος is the first criterion used by Aristotle to delineate the perimeter of the good. The ultimate end in Aristotle's worldview is god, the pure actuality of every potentiality. Teleology is a fundamental feature of every human action. Because every human is a political creature, this ultimate end is achieved by living in the city. This end is ultimate or best because there is nothing beyond it; it cannot be transcended, it is final and complete. This end is self-sufficient because it is a political reality. It can sustain itself because it is integrated in the self-sufficiency of the city. So, the frameworks of metaphysics and politics are needed to grasp the meaning of the criterion of finality.

Based on these facts Aristotle concludes one of his steps in investigating εὐδαιμονία: happiness, being final and self-sufficient, is the "End at which all actions aim" (*EN* I.7 1097b20). After drawing the first conclusion, Aristotle continues his analysis because we need a "more explicit account" of what happiness is (*EN* I.7 1097b23), and that can be attained by studying the function of man (*EN* I.7 1097b25).

4.3 ΕΥΔΑΙΜΟΝΙΑ AS ῎ΕΡΓΟΝ ᾿ΑΝΘΡΩΠΟΥ

In *EN* I.7 1098a21 Aristotle delineates for us a perimeter of the good [περιγεγράφθω τἀγαθὸν]. This action of "drawing a line around something" is what is needed for a "more explicit account of" happiness (*EN* I.7 1097b23). This "more explicit account" is obtained by inquiring into the function of man [τὸ ἔργον τοῦ ἀνθρώπου]. But as the first step in "delineating the perimeter" of the good, Aristotle brought forward the first "layer" of his inquiry, according to which happiness is something "final and self-sufficient, the end at which all actions aim" (*EN* I.7 1097b20). On this layer Aristotle brings the second one, that of the function of man, which is understood as "activity of the soul in accordance with excellence" [ψυχῆς ἐνέργεια γίνεται κατ᾿ ἀρετήν] (*EN* I.7 1098a20). Thus, the perimeter of the εὐδαιμονία is delineated with the help of the ultimate aim/τέλος and function of man/ἔργον ἀνθρώπου. The criteria of *finality* and *function* constitute the perimeter of the good of man; within that perimeter Aristotle can make affirmations about it.

In this section I investigate the criterion of function as part of Aristotle's perimeter of the good of man, or of εὐδαιμονία. The investigation has three main sections: 1) function of man/ἔργον ἀνθρώπου, 2) activity of the soul/ψυχῆς ἐνέργεια, 3) virtue/ἀρετή. These three sections are based on Aristotle's conclusion of the function argument in *EN* I.7 1198a15–20. The thesis of this chapter is that the function of man/ἔργον τοῦ ἀνθρώπου, in *EN*, is a metaphysical teleological concept and constitutes εὐδαιμονία, the good of man.

The first observation about this expression is its simplicity. Aristotle chooses a term to continue his inquiry on εὐδαιμονία: ἔργον (work, deed, activity). ῎Εργον is used by Aristotle to designate the work man is intended to do, its function. As he says, he is searching for the goodness or efficiency of an entity, and that is found in the function of that entity (*EN* I.7 1097b25). In Aristotle's words: ἐν τῷ ἔργῳ δοκεῖ τἀγαθὸν εἶναι ("the good is found in the function"; I.7 1097b28). This phrase is compact and not easy to understand. We are told about the activity in which we are finding the good of man, namely his work/function. I need to explore how Aristotle understands the function/work of an entity. From scholarly literature[63] I

---

63. The research done on the function of man in *EN* is vast. From the most recent titles I mention: Garver, "Human Function," 133–45; Achtenberg, "Ergon Argument," 59–72; Hester, "Function of Man"; Reeve, *Reason*, 123–28; Whiting, "Function Argument," 189–204; Tuozzo, "Function," 146–61.

will debate with Richard Kraut[64] who provides us with an extensive study on this topic. Kraut understands the function of man as contemplation and I will argue that the function is a metaphysical teleological concept, and it is the good of man.

4.3.1 Kraut on the function of man

Kraut's interpretative framework of the function of man argument is that of the "Aristotle's defense of the two lives"[65] (i.e., the life of virtues and the life of contemplation). According to Kraut, Aristotle argues that the "ethical virtues are intermediate states"[66] and the function argument is one part in the inquiry. The good in specialized spheres consists in fulfilling a certain function[67] and, based on this insight, Kraut says that this should be true about humans in general. Aristotle works with the criterion of peculiarity to identify our function as humans. Based on this criterion, Kraut says that "our function consists in contemplation."[68]

Kraut's defense of this conclusion is based on the observation that our function as humans "consists in something that sets us apart from plants and animals—rather than something that sets us apart from all living things whatsoever, including gods."[69] The function of man is something peculiar to us that "distinguishes us from other members of this class";[70] the class of humans, animals, and plants (*EN* I.7 1098a2). Because gods are superior to the humans, animals and plants, they are excluded from the comparison.[71] Aristotle takes for granted that the humans can live better lives than animals, and because they have an intermediate position, between animals and gods, our lives are somewhere between them too: "not as good as those of gods, and better than the lives of animals and plants."[72]

---

64. Kraut, *Human Good*.
65. Kraut, *Human Good*, 312.
66. Kraut, *Human Good*, 312.
67. Kraut, *Human Good*, 313.
68. Kraut, *Human Good*, 313.
69. Kraut, *Human Good*, 316.
70. Kraut, *Human Good*, 316.
71. Kraut, *Human Good*, 316.
72. Kraut, *Human Good*, 317.

The theory of the human good that Aristotle defends, according to Kraut, is that which "accords with this intermediate position."[73] Aristotle points to the kind of good is at the "top of the hierarchy of ends."[74] The function argument supports "the conclusion that one type of good deserves to be situated by itself at the pinnacle of human endeavors."[75] Kraut speaks about this good as "virtuous activity of the part of the soul that has reason."[76]

The overall perspective of Kraut's argument is that of the dominant position of εὐδαιμονία. From this perspective, the unity of the two lives, of virtue and contemplation, is always the focus of inquiry, and the function of man plays an important part in it. "The virtuous activity of the part of the soul that has reason" is, according to Kraut, the contemplation for which Aristotle will argue in *EN* X.6. Thus, *EN* I.7 and X.6 are part of the same overall argument.

Against Kraut I have several objections. First, even if Kraut offers a good analysis at the macro level of the entire *EN*, he does miss the layers of actual argument provided by Aristotle. The "function" argument is used by Aristotle to continue the inquiry at the point where the criterion of finality has left it. The function is studied because "the good is found in the function."[77] Aristotle can provide a "more explicit account of what constitutes happiness" (*EN* I.7 1097b22) by "ascertaining what is man's function" (*EN* I.7 1097b25). Heinaman makes a similar point when he says that "Aristotle has just given his function argument in order to achieve a more precise specification of *eudaimonia*."[78] But for Kraut, the function argument "is only one part of Aristotle's defense of the two lives" (the life of virtues and the life of contemplation). This is the macro-level effort of Kraut to focus on the unity of Aristotle's argument between *EN* I and *EN* X to defend a dominant interpretation of εὐδαιμονία.

Because of the fact that Kraut understands the function of man as contemplation, he needs to demonstrate at length why, then, the peculiarity of man is not understood against the gods, but only against the animals and plants, as Aristotle does in *EN* I.7. Kraut's argument focuses on what Aristotle says about the peculiarity of man; the human function "consists in

---

73. Kraut, *Human Good*, 317.

74. Kraut, *Human Good*, 317.

75. Kraut, *Human Good*, 319.

76. Kraut, *Human Good*, 319.

77. Kraut, *Human Good*, 312.

78. Heinaman, "Eudaimonia," 36.

something that sets us apart from plants and animals—rather than some-thing that sets us apart from all living things whatsoever, including gods";[79] (see also a similar analysis by Ackrill).[80] Kraut focuses so much on the unity of Aristotle's argument to argue for a dominant position of εὐδαιμονία that the actual place of function argument in Aristotle's text is no longer clear. In *EN* I.7, the function argument continues to delineate the perimeter of εὐδαιμονία, and in this perimeter the inquiry will bring in the "imprint" or the "form" of a happy life; this fundamental metaphysical teleological point is absent in Kraut's analysis because he misses the layers of Aristotle's inquiry.

The second objection is that Kraut does not offer an Aristotelian con-text for the idea of "function." Aristotle's function argument is short and sketchy, that is why it is necessary to integrate it in the larger Aristotelian framework by bringing in his ideas about the function from other places in his writing where he speaks about it. The basic question "what is the func-tion?" is left unanswered by Kraut. An inquiry on this aspect of Aristotle's thought leads the interpreter in the direction of biology and metaphysics. Aristotle expects the reader to have the basic knowledge about the idea of function on which s/he needs to build his/her reading of the text. The affir-mation from *EN* I.7 1097b28 that "the goodness [. . .] of anybody who has some function or business to perform is thought to reside in that function" is the basic presupposition that has to be explored in the larger Aristotelian framework of thought. The function argument is part of the inquiry be-cause it can elucidate the content of εὐδαιμονία, of the human good. This is metaphysical language that is left unexplored by Kraut.

Instead he focuses mainly on how the function serves at consolidating a dominant understanding of εὐδαιμονία. This is a classic example of how the interpreter's framework of thought dictates the way the text is read. As Kraut says: "the crucial part of the function argument is its attempt to support the conclusion that in fact one type of good [. . .] deserves to be situated by itself at the pinnacle of human endeavors."[81] This is so, accord-ing to Kraut, because Aristotle seeks "a theory of the human good," that ac-cords with the assumption that humans are intermediate beings (between animals and gods), and this intermediate position is better understood

---

79. Kraut, *Human Good*, 316.

80. Ackrill, "*Eudaimonia*," 70–72.

81. Kraut, *Human Good*, 319.

when we "discover which good is at the top of the hierarchy of ends."[82] These are the assumptions that make Kraut say that "our function consists in contemplation."[83]

The third objection against Kraut is that he leaves unexplored how the good of man resides in the function of man. Is the first part of the second? Are these two similar? If yes, in what way? If not, where is the difference? Aristotle's affirmation from *EN* I.7 1097b28: ἐν τῷ ἔργῳ δοκεῖ τἀγαθὸν εἶναι is a major metaphysical point. First is to be seen that the usual translation "reside" is not good enough; the term "reside" is not in the Greek text. Aristotle uses εἶναι and this term has to be translated with "is" (εἶναι is the present infinitive active of the verb εἰμί, "to be, to exist"). Thus, a better translation is: "it seems that the good *is* in the function," or, if we follow the Greek order of words, "in the function it seems the good *is*" (my italics). Aristotle does not say that the function exhausts the good, but that the function *is* where we have to look for the good of man.

His affirmation is bold and left unexplained. The reader is invited to explore more the Aristotelian stock of ideas to acquire a better grasp of that worldview. I understand Aristotle's affirmation as saying that the function of something is another way the good can be discerned. This kind of insight is similar with the previous ones from *EN* I, where Aristotle said that the good of man is his final end. The two are identical, the good and the final end, as these are, the good and the function.

4.3.2 What is the function?

The best way to proceed is to approach this second criterion of Aristotle's inquiry by seeing it in its place in the development of thought in *EN* and by elucidating the sketchy affirmations by exploring the larger Aristotelian framework of thought. Aristotle has to be interpreted with Aristotle. This is what I will do in this subsection, and then I will answer some possible objections to my thesis that the function, as a metaphysical teleological concept, is the good of man.

How does Aristotle understand the function of man? In *EN* I.7 he makes references to birth and peculiarity. Aristotle's affirmations in *EN* I.7 will guide us towards other Aristotelian texts to get the larger understanding of the function of man. The reference to man's birth [ἀργὸν πέφυκεν]

---

82. Kraut, *Human Good*, 317.

83. Kraut, *Human Good*, 313.

(*EN* I.7 1097b30) shows that the function of man is not something that is developed but that it is there from birth, is part of his nature. Aristotle asks if someone is "born without a function," and the answer that he gives is no. It is evident that different members of the human body have functions: the eye, the hand, the foot, etc. And then he asks, is the function of man is apart from all of these? Aristotle uses the criterion of peculiarity to answer this question. What is peculiar to man is the guide to identify the function of man (*EN* I.7 1098a2).

I argue that the function of something it is still part of the metaphysical inquiry about substance and being. This is in contrast to Kraut, and, as it will be shown later, it is in contrast to Korsgaard. The premise for my position is that for Aristotle substance and being are the main elements according to which all categories of being are referred; neither Kraut nor Korsgaard go with their analysis in this direction. But this is the direction to be followed because the concept of substance is the first part of everything there is (see my earlier argument in 4.2.2.2), and the category of being is divided in several ways and one of them is function: "individual things, quality, and quantity, and potency, complete reality, and of *function*" (my italics; *Met* IX.1045b).[84] This is the Aristotelian worldview and this is the place of "function" within it.

The concept of "function" is applied by Aristotle to any type of entity. For example, the Council of Athens has a variety of "functions." In the *Athenian Constitution* (part 49), Aristotle speaks about the cooperation between the Council and the magistrates and this is the last function on the list of the functions of that body. The Eleven [guardians] have the function, among others, of bringing "up information laid against magistrates alleged to be disqualified" (part 52,[85]). In the world of animals and plants, the function gives the distinction between the superior and inferior parts. The superior part is responsible for "distribution of nutriment and the process of growth" (*Gait of Animals*, part 4),[86] it is their starting point; for an animal it is the mouth, and for a plant it is the root. The mouth or the root have the function of nutriment and growth.

An important text in our inquiry is *Heavens* 2.3: "Everything which has a function exists for its function" [Ἕκαστόν ἐστιν, ὧν ἐστιν ἔργον, ἕνεκα

---

84. Ross, *Metaphysics*.
85. Rackham, *Aristotle*.
86. Farquharson, *On the Gait of Animals*.

τοῦ ἔργου].[87] The function of something gives the reason to be. The function is a metaphysical concept in that it delineates the way of existence for that entity. This discussion on function is integrated later in *Heavens* 3.8 when Aristotle says that "every natural body has, we maintain, its own functions, properties, and powers."[88] And this is to be understood in the general framework of Aristotelian metaphysics where "the final cause is the function" [οὗ δ᾽ ἕνεκα τὸ ἔργον] (*Met* III.2 996b).[89] The final cause is the aim of someone's existence. It is a teleological concept, it is the end and the good of a particular entity. Also, in *Meteorology* 4.12 Aristotle says that

> what a thing is, is always determined by its function: a thing really is itself when it can perform its function; an eye, for instance, when it can see. When a thing cannot do so, it is that thing only in name, like a dead eye or one made of stone.[90]

According to Aristotle, "all things are defined by their function and capacity" [πάντα δὲ τῷ ἔργῳ ὥρισται καὶ τῇ δυνάμει] (*Pol* I.1 1253a).[91]

These essential affirmations give us the broader framework in which to interpret what Aristotle says in *EN* I.7 1097b28: ἐν τῷ ἔργῳ δοκεῖ τἀγαθὸν εἶναι ("it seems that in the function the good is"). The function is a category of being, it is applied to every entity, "everything which has a function exists for that function." Richardson Lear echoes this point when she says that "the point is that where there is a function, all other typical capacities and activities are worth choosing for its sake."[92] The aim of someone's existence "is the function it fulfills," and the function is the factor that determines what a thing is.[93] Based on these fundamental observations I argue that the good is the function. Bush speaks about the relationships between these two in terms of correspondence: "the human good corresponds to the human function,"[94] and he also says that "the human function determines the human good."[95] The human function and the human good are identical;

---

87. Stocks, *On the Heavens.*
88. Stocks, *On the Heavens.*
89. Tredennick, *Aristotle.*
90. Webster, *Meteorology.*
91. Rackham, *Aristotle.*
92. Richardson Lear, *Happy Lives and the Highest Good*, 44.
93. See also Nagel, "Aristotle on *Eudaimonia*," 253.
94. Bush, "Happiness," 62.
95. Bush, "Happiness," 64.

the one is found in the other. The function as a metaphysical concept, is the good of man. This understanding of the function in terms of the good is elucidated by Aristotle by bringing the ἀρετή into the definition of the function, as we shall see later in 4.3.6.

This interpretation of function goes against that defended by Hardie who says that "the notion of function cannot be defended and should not be pressed, since a man is not designed for a purpose."[96] Kenny says the same thing: "we need not credit Aristotle with believing that men serve a purpose."[97] A more recent supporter of Hardie is Tuozzo who says that the texts that support a metaphysical claim are providing an "extremely weak support for the claim."[98] Hardie's position shows a lack of understanding of Aristotle's worldview, where the concept of function is an integral prominent part. Hardie's own presuppositions and interpretation of Aristotle, which exclude the possibility of metaphysical teleological understanding of function, cause him to redefine "function of man" strictly in terms of "the specific nature of man,"[99] and from there he defends a "narrower conception" of the proper function of man. His example shows, again, how the secular inclusive/dominant debate absorbed the research on εὐδαιμονία and every element of Aristotle's inquiry was used to defend one of these major positions. This can be seen when Hardie says that "this notion [function of man] can be given a wider interpretation which corresponds to the inclusive end or a narrower interpretation which corresponds to the dominant end."[100] In Hardie's case, Aristotle is not allowed to speak with his own voice (teleological metaphysics of the function is left aside), or his voice is redefined in strict naturalistic terms (the function of man interpreted in terms of specific nature of man).

My understanding of the function of man argued for here has one potential weakness, and that is that Aristotle says that "the good is *in* the function" (*EN* I.7 1097b28). The preposition "in" can mean that the good is [to be found] in the function,[101] with the implication that the concept of the function does not exhaust the concept of the good. There is something more in the function than the good is.

---

96. Hardie, "Final Good," 280.

97. Kenny, "Happiness," 96.

98. Tuozzo, "Function," 147.

99. Hardie, "Final Good," 280.

100. Hardie, "Final Good," 280 See also Ackrill, "*Eudaimonia*," 70.

101. Muresan, *Etica Nicomahica*, 61.

In *EN* I.7 1097b28 Aristotle says: ἐν τῷ ἔργῳ δοκεῖ τἀγαθὸν εἶναι ("*in the function it seems the good is*"). Aristotle does not say that the good is in the function in an absolute way, but that it is "*in the function.*" In other words, the function is the *locus* of the good. I understand this as an affirmation of identification: the function is what the good is. And, as the other texts I discussed above show, the function of an entity, according to Aristotle, has this role of identifying, giving the reason to be, defining what a thing is.

4.3.3 The function argument

Now, after I established "what the function is," I have to explore the function argument itself and its two major components, the activity of the soul and excellence. I will argue that the function of man done well corresponds to the good of man.

Aristotle works with a known view according to which there is a correspondence between goodness and function. The general premise of the argument is

(P1)—if the goodness of anybody who has some function is thought to be in that function, then, the conclusion follows

(C)—the good of man is in the function of man.

Aristotle has to establish that man has a function, and, if he has, what that function is. He observes that every member of the human body has its own function: the eye, the hand, the foot (*EN* I.7 1097b32), and then, he asks: "Does a human being also have a certain function over and above all the functions of his particular members?" (*EN* I.7 1097b33). This argument, the first move in the "function argument," is based on the premise:

(P1) every bodily part has its function,

(C) thus, a human being has a certain function apart from all of these.

The second move is to explore what the special function of man is (*EN* I.7 1097b34). Aristotle searches for what is peculiar to man in comparison with other earthly living things, like plants and animals. He identifies and discusses three types of lives: nutrition and growth, sense perceptions, and action. The human being shares the life of nutrition and growth with plants, and the life of sense perception is shared with animals (horses, oxen, etc.) but the life of action or the practical life of the rational part of man [πρακτιχή τις τοῦ λόγον ἔχοντος] (*EN* I.7 1098a4) is peculiar to man among the earthly species of living things. This type of life is the object of further investigation. Aristotle's argument has several premises (which are coined as conditionals) and one conclusion (*EN* I.7 1098a10–17):

P1—"if the function of man is the active exercise of the soul's faculties in conformity with rational principle"

P2—"if [. . .] the function of an individual and of a good individual of the same class to be generically the same"

P3—"if [. . .] the function of man is a certain form of life [. . .] (the exercise of the soul's faculties and activities in association with rational principle)"

P4—[if] "the function of a good man is to perform these activities well and rightly"

P5—"if a function is well performed when it is performed in accordance with its own proper excellence"

C—"then, it follows that the good of man is the active exercise of his soul's faculties in conformity with excellence" [τὸ ἀθρώπινον ἀγαθὸν ψυχῆς ἐνέργεια γίνεται κατ' ἀρετήν]

These five premises build an argument on the identification of the function of man as the active exercise of the soul's faculties in conformity with rational principle, and add the facts that for both an individual and a good individual the function stays the same, and that the function is a certain form of life, and the function of a good man is to perform well and rightly the activities of the soul, and when the function is well performed, it is performed in accordance with excellence. Thus, based on these premises, which focus on the function of man, Aristotle reaches the conclusion about the good of man as the activity of the soul in accordance with excellence. Thus, the function of man performed well corresponds to the good of man. Based on this, I see εὐδαιμονία, the good of man, as *the function of man performed well*.

4.3.4 Korsgaard on function and virtue

But I need to unpack this criterion of function. My focus is on the two major parts of Aristotle's conclusion: ψυχῆς ἐνέργεια (activity of the soul) and κατ' ἀρετήν (in accordance with excellence). These two components are of great importance in my inquiry into the meaning of εὐδαιμονία in *EN*. From the scholarly literature I will present and analyze the works of Christine Korsgaard (1986) and Julia Annas (1999) as the major interlocutors in this section.

Korsgaard's study "Aristotle on Function and Virtue" is an inquiry in moral virtue. Specifically, she investigates how the virtues (moral and intellectual) make us good at rational activity.[102] Korsgaard understands the role of the "function argument" as "the basis of Aristotle's theory of virtues."[103] The virtues are integrated into the fulfilling of the function. This perspective posits a strong bond between human rational activity and human virtues. The presence of the human virtues helps the rational activity to improve.

How is this taking place? The way Korsgaard approaches this question is by noting that the moral virtue is "a state of character, concerned with choice, lying in a mean."[104] These fundamental aspects of character, choice, and the mean are the pillars of Korsgaard's inquiry. Korsgaard's answer integrates them by focusing on the presence of the disposition in a way that is good for the rational activity. Someone has to be in "a good condition" for having the virtues improving the rational activity.[105] In this way the "good condition" relates to the appetitive part of the soul because this part of the soul has a rational factor; when is the appetitive part of the soul in a good condition? Korsgaard analyses different answers/theories (obedience,[106]

---

102. Korsgaard, "Function and Virtue," 260.

103. Korsgaard, "Function and Virtue," 260.

104. Korsgaard, "Function and Virtue," 261.

105. Korsgaard, "Function and Virtue," 262.

106. 'The appetitive part of the soul is in a good condition for rational activity when the passions give way to reason' (Korsgaard, "Function and Virtue," 262).

harmony,[107] susceptibility of argument,[108] health analogy,[109] perception,[110]) and, then, offers her answer, which is a combination of the perception theory with the health analogy and susceptibility of argument theory.[111]

For Korsgaard, what gives health to the human soul is the "susceptibility to argument,"[112] the condition in which someone's virtues make him or her good at the formulation and execution of rational plans. This good condition is provided and maintained by the moral virtues.[113] Such a person finds pleasure in what s/he does, and that preserves "the argument-susceptible condition"; what is pleasurable and judged to be good keeps the reason in control of the soul.[114] When the soul reaches the potential for rational activity is when the good of the soul is reached. Thus, what is morally good is what is good for the soul, and that is when the soul reaches the full potential for rational activity.[115]

Based on this, virtue is "the state in which a human being can perceive correctly, and be motivated by, considerations of what is noble and good, and so can engage in rational activity."[116] Korsgaard says that in the life of such a virtuous person the desires and emotions are caused by the dictates of reason, and s/he "prefers and chooses those actions that maintain this condition."[117]

---

107. "The appetitive part of the soul is in a good condition for rational activity when the desires and emotions are in harmony with the dictates of reason" (Korsgaard, "Function and Virtue," 262).

108. "The appetitive part of the soul is in a good condition for rational activity when the desires and emotions are caused by rational considerations" (Korsgaard, "Function and Virtue," 262).

109. "Moral virtues are qualities that in general way make one good at formulation and execution of rational plans and projects; their relation to rational activity is analogous to the relation of the physical virtues to physical activity" (Korsgaard, "Function and Virtue," 262–63).

110. "The appetitive part of the soul is in a good condition for rational activity when what we perceive to be good really is good: because we perceive evaluative qualities correctly we are able to make correct judgments about evaluative issues" (Korsgaard, "Function and Virtue," 263).

111. Korsgaard, "Function and Virtue," 275.

112. Korsgaard, "Function and Virtue," 276.

113. Korsgaard, "Function and Virtue," 276.

114. Korsgaard, "Function and Virtue," 276.

115. Korsgaard, "Function and Virtue," 276.

116. Korsgaard, "Function and Virtue," 277.

117. Korsgaard, "Function and Virtue," 277.

Reason can be corrupted, that is why someone's practical reason functions well when that person is virtuous; the virtues help that person "to form a correct conception of what is good for the soul."[118] Korsgaard says that for Aristotle, reason is a "potentiality that may or may not come out right, depending upon the condition one is in." Someone cannot reach his/her full potential without the moral virtues. The moral virtues "actualize our potential for rationality."[119] Korsgaard position will be evaluated later, after I present Annas's interpretation about virtue and happiness.

4.3.5 Annas on virtue and happiness

Annas provides a study of virtue in *EN* by focusing on the idea that virtue is not sufficient for happiness.[120] She inquires how the reader of *EN* can integrate this problematic idea (that virtue is not sufficient for happiness) with the Aristotle's overall conception of happiness.

Annas understands the ethical theory of Aristotle as starting "from the notion of our having a final good, an inclusive and unifying aim that structures what we do."[121] Happiness is the final aim based on the ground that meets some conditions for something to be a final good: completeness, self-sufficient, and most choiceworthy.[122] These aspects of the final good make the notion of happiness more precise and formal.[123] These are the criteria used by Aristotle to evaluate any candidate for happiness. He concludes that happiness is "a life of virtuous activity, along with adequate external goods."[124] The mention of external goods makes Aristotle committed to the idea that the virtuous life is not complete and self-sufficient on its own.[125]

Annas's work is important for this section because she explores the link between the virtues and the affective side of man. Aristotelian virtues are settled states of character that have an affective side:[126] to have a virtue

---

118. Korsgaard, "Function and Virtue," 277.

119. Korsgaard, "Function and Virtue," 278.

120. Annas, "Virtue and Happiness," 35.

121. Annas, "Virtue and Happiness," 36.

122. Annas, "Virtue and Happiness," 36.

123. Annas, "Virtue and Happiness," 36.

124. Annas, "Virtue and Happiness," 37.

125. Annas, "Virtue and Happiness," 37.

126. Annas, "Virtue and Happiness," 37.

is "to have one's relevant motivation habituated and trained in the right direction."[127] This is how Annas understands the complex phrase the activity of the soul according to virtue/ψυχῆς ἐνέργεια γίνεται κατ' ἀρετήν (*EN* I.7 1098a17). The virtues are at such a stage in someone's life that s/he does not have to fight desires countering right action. These opposing desires have not developed to go in the direction of virtue, or against it.[128] In this state, this person takes pleasure in being virtuous. The point of all this is that the agent judges and does the right action and has no motivation not to do it.[129]

The virtuous person is a person in which virtues are fully developed and the activity of the soul is always according to ἀρετή. This person enjoys how and what s/he does. For Aristotle, according to Annas, these are the components of a "unified personality": virtue (with its dispositional and affective sides) and pleasure (positive attitude and enjoyment);[130] in the virtuous person's psychological world "the claims of everything but virtue is silenced by virtue."[131]

Then, Annas explores the "cognitive side of virtue" in saying that a fully virtuous person has developed practical reason.[132] Such a person does not need to work out every time what the right action is to perform, because s/he will just "see what in the situation is morally relevant."[133] This is so, because the Aristotelian virtuous person is not tempted to do otherwise. S/he has a "clear view of what virtue requires"; and s/he performs what virtue requires for its own sake.[134] For someone to be and act like that it means that her/his judgment and emotions are fully transformed; s/he is "single-minded" in the direction of virtue.[135]

This understanding of the virtuous person is then analyzed by Annas, in relation to the external goods. Her question is: Why is such a life not complete and self-sufficient? Why does it need some external goods?[136]

127. Annas, "Virtue and Happiness," 37.
128. Annas, "Virtue and Happiness," 38.
129. Annas, "Virtue and Happiness," 38.
130. Annas, "Virtue and Happiness," 39.
131. Annas, "Virtue and Happiness," 39.
132. Annas, "Virtue and Happiness," 39.
133. Annas, "Virtue and Happiness," 39.
134. Annas, "Virtue and Happiness," 39.
135. Annas, "Virtue and Happiness," 40.
136. Annas, "Virtue and Happiness," 40.

The remaining part of Annas" article explores this dilemma. I analyzed the "happiness and the external goods" debate in 2.3.3, and I will develop my answer in 5.5, so I will not explore it here. Annas' conclusion is that Aristotle "has no obvious way of reconciling these two"; he both says that happiness is complete, and that the external goods are needed for happiness.[137] According to Annas, Aristotle reflects the fact that there is a problem, and that it is not "the task of his ethical theory to solve it."[138]

I criticize Korsgaard and Annas from the point of view of my thesis in this chapter. I argue that the "function of man," in *EN*, is a metaphysical teleological concept, and as such, it is the good of man. My first objection is that both Korsgaard and Annas for explaining the idea of function they need to provide what Aristotle thinks about it. To explain the Aristotelian idea of function the interpreter needs to make reference to the larger metaphysical framework (see especially *Heavens* 2.3, 3.8; *Met* III.2; *Meteorology* 4.2; *Pol* I.1 1253a) that is at work here. Annas integrates her analysis in the larger teleological framework of εὐδαιμονία but the function argument needs more than that, as I have shown earlier (see the section 4.3.2).

My second objection against Korsgaard and Annas is that they do not explore the particularities of Aristotle's understanding of the soul in *EN* [Ἔργον ἀνθρώπου ψυχῆς ἐνέργεια κατὰ λόγον] (*EN* I.7 1098a7). Aristotle introduces the concept of the soul into his inquiry when he discusses in what sense different things are called good. His answer is that things are called good because they contribute to good by way of a proportion (*EN* I.6 1096b29). He illustrates this by saying: "that is, as sight is good in the body, so reason is good in the soul" [ὡς ἐν σώματι ὄψις, ἐν ψυχῇ νοῦς] (*EN* I.6 1096b29).

The point of interest for this project is the way Aristotle explains some complex relationships: sight-body and reason-soul. These two are similarly related to each other. The body and the soul have sight and mind within them, and both of these are the "good." Aristotle does not explore further this saying because, he says, it belongs to "another branch of philosophy" (*EN* I.6 1096b32; i.e. First Philosophy or Metaphysics). But for my argument this is exactly what the reader needs: the awareness of a metaphysical perspective when Aristotle approaches the concepts of the good and the soul. Only in this way the reader can put together, in the way Aristotle wanted, the whole picture of his inquiry when he says that τὸ ἀνθρώπινον

137. Annas, "Virtue and Happiness," 47.
138. Annas, "Virtue and Happiness," 47.

ἀγαθόν ψυχῆς ἐνέργεια γίνεται κατ' ἀρετήν (the good of man is the activity of the soul according to excellence, *EN* I.7 1098a17) where the concepts of "the good" and "the soul" came together in the definition of εὐδαιμονία. At the end of unpacking the criterion of ἔργον ἀνθρώπου (with the focus on the activity of the soul and on the virtues) Aristotle says that εὐδαιμονία requires "both complete goodness and complete lifetime" (*EN* I.9 1100a5).

My third objection against Korsgaard and Annas is that they do not offer an explanation of why Aristotle chooses κατὰ λόγον (according to rational principle) and not κατὰ νοῦν (according to intelligence/mind/thought) in his definition of the function of man. Is there a reason for this? And how important is the reference to κατὰ λόγον, when at the end of the function argument the phrase is no longer part of the formula, and it seems to be replaced by the phrase κατ' ἀρετήν (according to virtue/excellence; *EN* I.7 1098a17)? Is no longer "the rational principle" needed? Or ψυχῆς ἐνέργεια is a technical phrase that includes in its meaning the unmentioned κατὰ λόγον? I incline to read the text as such based on the importance of the rational choice focused on "the mean" that follows later in Aristotle's inquiry (*EN* II.2 1104a26, VI.1 1138b19), and because the happy man will be "most often employed in doing and contemplating the things that are in conformity with virtue" (*EN* I.10 1100b19). Rational activity and virtue go together, they are not exclusive of each other.

After examining the main interlocutors, Korsgaard and Annas, I need to focus myself on the major Aristotelian phrase in *EN* I.7 1098a17 which defines the good of man: τὸ ἀνθρώπινον ἀγαθόν ψυχῆς ἐνέργεια γίνεται κατ' ἀρετήν (the good of man is the activity of the soul according to excellence). This is the studied in the next section.

4.3.6 Activity of the soul according to virtue

According to Aristotle, the good of man is an activity of the soul. That is why in this section I need to focus first on what Aristotle has to say about the soul. I will do this by studying the larger Aristotelian understanding of the soul and its elements, then by exploring the meaning of the key phrase ψυχῆς ἐνέργεια (the activity of the soul), and, at the end of the section, I will explore the meaning ἀρετή.

Aristotle introduces the soul into his inquiry rather abruptly. His other mention of it before *EN* I.7 in the definition of the function of the man as the "activity of the soul," is in *EN* I.6 1096b29: "as sight is in the body, so is reason in the soul" [ὡς γὰρ ἐν σώματι ὄψις, ἐν ψυχῇ νοῦς]. This reference to the soul explains how I will interpret the relation between reason and soul and position myself in the debate with Korsgaard and Annas.

Sight and body is the model for understanding reason and soul. Sight offers guidance to the body, it offers another link to the surrounding world besides the other senses. The relationship between sight and body is complex. And therefore, so will be the relationship between reason and soul. For man to function well it needs his soul to follow a rational principle. The overall understanding of the soul's components is given in *EN* II.5 1105a20, where Aristotle says that "things that are found in the soul are of three kinds—passions, faculties, states of character" [πάθη, δυνάμεις ἕξεις]. This is the general outlook we need for explaining the "activity of the soul" both in relation to the rational principle and virtue.

In the soul, Aristotle says, there are several elements: one irrational element is the one that is vegetative in nature and causes nutrition and growth (*EN* I.13 1102b1). Another irrational element in the soul is the one that "shares in a rational principle" [μετέχουσα μέντοι πῃ λόγου] (*EN* I.13 1102b13). The man who shows self-restraint, in contrast with the man who does not show it, is an example of someone in whom the rational principle is at work. The rational principle, in which an element of the soul shares, has the ability to urge the soul aright towards the best objects (*EN* I.13 1102b16). When the soul of someone is moved astray into the opposite direction a man becomes incontinent and, in his soul, "something contrary to the rational principle" [ἀντιτείνει τῷ λόγῳ] (*EN* I.13 1102b17)[139] resists and opposes. There is a "justice" between certain parts of every human being, a "justice" similar to that between "a master and servant" (*EN* V.11 1138b8). "These are the ratios in which the part of the soul that has a rational principle stands to the irrational part" [διέστηκε τὸ λόγον ἔχον μέρος τῆς ψυχῆς πρὸς τὸ ἄλογον] (*EN* V.11 1138b9). It has to be "a mutual justice between them as between ruler and ruled" (*EN* V.11 1138b13).

The rational part of the soul is again divided in two: with one we "contemplate those things whose first principles are invariable," and with the other we "contemplate those things which admit variation" (*EN* VI.1 1139a8). Aristotle labels these two faculties as the "scientific faculty" and the "calculative faculty" (*EN* VI.1 1139a15). Neither Korsgaard nor Annas touches on these aspects of Aristotelian psychology in their accounts of soul and virtue. The activity of contemplation, understood with the object

139. Ross, *Nicomachean Ethics.*

of contemplation in view, is important for my argument because the last layer of Aristotle's inquiry is also that of contemplation; there is this common ground of contemplation between the ἔργον ἀνθρώπου and θεώρια in Aristotle's inquiry on εὐδαιμονία. Contemplating the first principles that are invariable and the things that admit variation are different activities of the soul. The excellency/virtue of these two faculties (scientific and calculative) is given by their function [ἡ δ" ἀρετὴ πρὸς τὸ ἔργον τὸ οἰκεῖον] "the virtue of a faculty is related to the special function which that faculty performs" *EN* VI.2 1139a18).

To explain how someone is triggered to action, Aristotle goes deeper into the soul and says that in it there are three elements that control action and the attainment of truth: sensation, intellect, and desire [αἴσθησις, νοῦς, ὄρεξις] (*EN* VI.2 1139a19). The cause of action is choice, and the "cause of choice is desire and reasoning directed to some end" (*EN* VI.2 1139a34). This teleological understanding of choice makes Aristotle to bring together thought and dispositions of character; no one can do well without thought and character (*EN* VI.2 1139a35). The aspect of interest for us is the "activity of the soul" as this is related to active exercise/action. Here again, Aristotle uses a metaphysical framework: "thought by itself moves nothing, but only thought directed to an end, and dealing with action" (*EN* VI.2 1139a36). These are echoes of his argument from *Metaphysics* XI about the unmoved mover who moves everything by the power of teleological thought/thought directed to an end.

But there is an explicit (metaphysical) link between ἐνέργεια and εὐδαιμονία in *Met* IX.1050a35-b2:

> where there is no other result besides the actualization [τὴν ἐνέργειαν], the actualization [ἡ ἐνέργεια] resides in the subject; e.g., seeing in the seer, and speculation [ἡ θεωρία] in the speculator [τῷ θεωροῦντα], and life in the soul (and hence also happiness [ἡ εὐδαιμονία], since happiness is a particular kind of life).[140]

This explicit link in Aristotle's metaphysics between ἐνέργεια and εὐδαιμονία, as far as I am aware, is not explored by other scholars in their research concerning the meaning of εὐδαιμονία in *EN*. The only scholarly mention of *Met* IX about ἐνέργεια and the research concerning the human good in Aristotle, that I am aware of, is that of Nussbaum when she says that

---

140. Tredennick, *Aristotle*.

we might think in this connection [of *energeia versus kinesis*] of the *Metaphysics* Book IX distinction of the broad class of *energeiai* into two subclasses—the class of *kineseis*, "motions," and the (narrow) class of *energeiai*. *Energeiai* (narrowly construed) are activities that are complete at any moment: they "have their form in themselves."[141]

I build on this important observation by Nussbaum by mentioning Aristotle's two distinctions between potentiality and actuality, and motion and actuality, in *Met* IX. Aristotle distinguishes between potentiality and actuality of an entity by using an antithesis: "that as that which is actually building is to that which is capable of building" (*Met* IX.1048a35). Actuality and potentiality are defined by these two members of the antithesis, the first being the actuality and the second being the potentiality of building. And then, Aristotle distinguishes between motion and actuality by saying that

> every motion is incomplete—the process of thinning, learning, walking, building—these are motions, and incomplete at that. For it is not the same thing which at the same time is walking and has walked, or is building and has built, or is becoming and has become, [. . .]; the latter kind of process, then, is what I mean by actualization [ἐνέργειαν], and the former what I mean by motion [κίνησιν]. (*Met* IX.1048b35)[142]

Thus, the Greek term ἐνέργεια, in the philosophy of Aristotle, when opposed to "potentiality" [δύναμις], means "actuality."[143] It can be seen in the above explanations that Aristotle has a specific usage of the term ἐνέργεια and it is best translated with "actuality." When I apply this explicit metaphysical link between ἐνέργεια and εὐδαιμονία to Aristotle's definition of εὐδαιμονία as ψυχῆς ἐνέργεια (*EN* I.7 1098a17), the whole inquiry is seen in a different light. Εὐδαιμονία as ἐνέργεια is a metaphysical entity; it is the "actuality/active exercise of the soul," it is *the soul reaching actuality*. So, these are the major points about the "activity of the soul" in *EN*; and we need to understand them because "the function of man is an activity of the soul which follows a rational principle" (*EN* I.7 1098a7).

Now, we need to explore more the phrase κατὰ λόγον (following/according to rational principle). The phrase itself occurs several times in *EN* (I.3 1095a; I.7 1098a; I.10 1100a; I.10 1101a; IX.8 1169a). Besides *EN* I.7

---

141. Nussbaum, *Fragility*, 326.

142. Tredennick, *Aristotle*.

143. Liddell, Scott, Jones, and Mckenzie, *A Greek-English Lexicon*, 564.

1098a7, the occurrence from *EN* IX.8 1169a5 is of relevance to my study. There Aristotle speaks about the good man and says:

> the good man will be a lover of self in the fullest degree, though in another sense than a lover of self so-called by way of reproach, from whom he differs as much as living by principle [κατὰ λόγον] differs from living by passion and aiming at what is noble from aiming at what seems expedient.[144]

The good man is a man that "takes for himself the things that are noblest and most truly good" (*EN* IX.8 1169a5); because he obeys "the most dominant part of himself," he is a "lover of self in the fullest degree." This is seen in our "reasoned acts that are felt to be in the fullest sense our own acts." Thus, "living by principle" [τὸ κατὰ λόγον ζῆν] (*EN* IX.8 1169a5) is living by obeying the most dominant part of us, which is ourselves, and this leads to aiming, for ourselves, at things that are most noble and truly good. A good man "ought to be a lover of self" (*EN* IX.8 1169a12). Aiming at the most noble and good is living by (rational) principle; this is seen when our intellect makes us to choose the best, to be self-restrained and leads to "reasoned acts."

Thus, κατὰ λόγον is a phrase through which Aristotle underlies the dominant role of rational principle in guiding our aims. Our intellect aims us towards what is most noble and most good. And, in *EN*, this is εὐδαιμονία, the ultimate most good of man.

This action of the soul according to rational principle is further refined by Aristotle using the phrase κατ᾽ ἀρετήν (according to virtue/excellence, *EN* I.7 1098a17). Ἀρετή has a similar role with λόγος; it is an element of influence, it has the power to guide the activity of the soul towards the ultimate most good.

The next step of my inquiry is to explain what ἀρετή means for Aristotle in *EN*. Virtue is mentioned for the first time in *EN* in I.5 1095b29: "virtue is a greater good than honor." Then, when compared with εὐδαιμονία, it does not pass the test of completeness to be the end of man; this is so because "it is possible to possess it while you are asleep" (*EN* I.5 1095b32). Also, excellence in all its forms is chosen for its own sake (*EN* I.7 1097b3). Nonetheless, to understand εὐδαιμονία, ἀρετή is important. This is so because the function of man presupposes it: "the good of man is the active

---

144. Rackham, *Nicomachean Ethics*.

exercise of his soul's faculties in conformity with excellence or virtue" (*EN* I.7 1098a17).

This affirmation is reiterated by Aristotle in *EN* I.13 1102a5 as the starting point for studying ἀρετή: "inasmuch as happiness is a certain activity of soul in conformity with perfect goodness/virtue, it is necessary to examine the nature of goodness/virtue." The study of ἀρετή is another aspect that needs to be covered in the larger inquiry on εὐδαιμονία. Both εὐδαιμονία and ἀρετή are related to the soul; the first is an "activity of the soul" and the second is the "excellence of the soul" (*EN* I.13 1102a16). This is why a study of the "nature of the soul" is needed (*EN* I.13 1102a25).

I already covered these aspects related to the soul in the first part of this section. The soul consists of two parts, one irrational (vegetative that causes nutrition and growth, and appetites and desire) and the other capable of reason (*EN* I.13 1102a29). The appetitive part participates in the rational part as being obedient to it (*EN* I.13 1102b32). Virtue is also differentiated in "correspondence with this division of the soul:" "intellectual virtues" (wisdom, intelligence, prudence) and "moral virtues" (liberality, temperance) (*EN* I.13 1103a5–7). The intellectual virtues are produced and increased by instruction, and moral virtues are the product of habit (*EN* II.1 1103a15–16). The moral virtues are no part of our nature, but our nature gives us the capacity to acquire them (*EN* II.1 1103a25). We acquire virtues by practicing them; we become just by doing just acts (*EN* II.1 1103b1).

At this point in his inquiry (*EN* II.2 1104a11) Aristotle reminds us that this type of discussion is "inexact" because things of conduct have nothing fixed and invariable about them (*EN* II.2 1104a5). He guides the analysis towards an understanding of "how we are to act rightly" (*EN* II.2 1103b30). This is understood as "acting in conformity with right principle" (*EN* II.2 1103b32) and "observing the mean" (*EN* II.2 1104a26). This gives the path towards preserving and enhancing our moral qualities. Excess and deficiency destroy the moral qualities. The same actions can both generate and foster the virtues, they also can destroy them (if the mean is not observed), but also the virtues will find "their full exercise in the same actions" (*EN* II.2 1104a28). Aristotle says that "moral virtue" [ἠθικὴ ἀρετή] is concerned with "pleasures and pains" (*EN* II.3 1104b9) and gives several reasons for this (see details in *EN* II.3. 1104b14—1105a7). Acts themselves and the agent him- or herself have to be of a certain sort: the first, "in conformity with virtues," and second, "in a certain state of mind" (act with knowledge, choose to act for its own sake, the disposition of character is the source of his action) (*EN* II.4 1105a32–34). The repeated performance of just and temperate acts results in virtue (*EN* II.4 1105b4).

Aristotle sees virtues as "dispositions"; the text that brings together the good of man, the function of man, and virtue is *EN* II.6 1106a24: "virtue in a man will be the disposition which renders him a good man and also which will cause him to perform his function well." These dispositions are "formed states of character in virtue of which we are well or ill-disposed in respect of the emotions" (*EN* II.5 1105b25). This definition is explored further on the premise that "all excellence has a twofold effect on the thing to which it belongs": it renders their goodness and causes their well-functioning (*EN* II.6 1106a17). As the man is concerned, excellence will do the same: it renders him a good man and causes him to perform his function well. Thus, virtue is "a mean state" (*EN* II.6 1106b27), a "settled disposition of the mind" (*EN* II.6 1106b35) between two vices; it does not either "fall short of or exceed what is right" (*EN* II.6 1106b17).[145] That is why it is not an easy task to be good; it is hard "to find the middle point in anything" (*EN* II.9 1109a25). The examples of some particular virtues and vices given by Aristotle are as follows (his detailed analysis is given in *EN* II.7 1107a30–1108b9): courage is the mean between fear and confidence, temperance is the mean between pleasures and pains, liberality is the mean between giving and getting money, and the greatness of soul is the mean between honor and dishonor. Truthfulness is the mean in respect of truth, wittiness is the mean in respect of pleasantness, and friendliness is the mean in respect of general pleasantness in life.

Aristotle provides three rules in "aiming at the mean:" to avoid the extremes which are more opposed to the mean, to notice what are the errors to which we are ourselves most prone, and to guard against what is pleasant and against pleasure (see *EN* II.8 1108b20–35). Thus, aiming at the mean is about intermediacy. Someone ought to choose "not the excess nor the defect" (*EN* VI.1 1138b19). Choosing what is equally removed from the two opposite is a "just action" (*EN* V.5 1133b30).[146] Someone's activity has to be marked by this standard found "between excess and defect" (*EN* VI.1 1138b25).

Thus, virtue as disposition is the platform both for rendering a man as being good, and for making him fulfill his function well. This is the activity

---

145. Ross, *Nicomachean Ethics*.
146. Ross, *Nicomachean Ethics*.

of the soul according to virtue, the second layer of Aristotle's inquiry on εὐδαιμονία. This is how the good is the function.

4.4 CONCLUSION

My argument in this chapter is that Aristotle uses the criteria of finality and function to delineate the perimeter of the good. The good of man, εὐδαιμονία, is the ultimate end of every human being. In Aristotle's world-view, the ultimate aim is a metaphysical concept which is understood in terms of actuality in which every potentiality reaches its completion. The unmoved mover, god, the pure actuality, is the ultimate aim of entire universe. God as νοῦς is the climax of everything there is, as everything is attracted by it, as everything tends to go towards this supreme aim. Thus, according to the criterion of finality εὐδαιμονία is this ultimate end, the actuality of our soul according to reason. This good of man, the actuality of man is the end by excellence; there is nothing beyond it, it is ultimate. No human being can use this ultimate end to achieve something beyond it. Also, this ultimate aim of every human being is self-sufficient because it is a political reality. Every human being is a social/political being. The life s/he lives is lived in a city. The sufficiency of the city is the foundation for the sufficiency of εὐδαιμονία. Actuality as the ultimate end is achieved in the city.

To further elucidate the meaning of εὐδαιμονία, Aristotle works with the criterion of function. The function of something in Aristotle's worldview is a metaphysical teleological concept which describes the thing or the act something/someone has to perform to find or fulfill its/his/her meaning. This function of something/someone is the good of it. In Aristotle's own words: "in the function . . . the good is." The human function and the human good are identical. The function of an entity, according to Aristotle, has the role of identifying, giving the reason to be, and defining what that entity is. Aristotle identifies the function of man as being the actuality of the soul according to rational principle and according to virtue. When our intellect and our virtues guide the soul towards the ultimate good, our soul reaches actuality, it fulfills its function. Virtue as disposition makes a human being to fulfill his/her function well. This is how the good is in the function.

With these two criteria Aristotle delineates the perimeter of the good. This delineation is metaphysical and teleological. This perimeter shows how integrated Aristotle's metaphysics and ethics are. Both of them are teleological and ethics is embedded in metaphysics. But Aristotle will continue to explore the function argument in *EN* X.6–8 by following it teleologically all the way up to the complete happiness. The function criterion is explored further by focusing on the "highest part of us," our intellect. The actuality/activity of the highest part of us, θεώρια is studied in the next chapter.

CHAPTER 5

THE IMPRINT OF
HAPPINESS COMPLETED
IN CONTEMPLATION

5.1 INTRODUCTION

In CHAPTER 1, I stated that my thesis about the meaning of εὐδαιμονία in *EN* is that Aristotle understands εὐδαιμονία as actuality through the help of two major phrases: "perimeter of the good" and "imprint of happiness." "Εὐδαιμονία as actuality" is the ultimate point in the process of reaching the ultimate aim of humanity; it is the point at which we reach the maximum of our potentiality. In Chapter 2, I presented an overview of Aristotle's ethical inquiry. Then, I discussed the three classic puzzles about the meaning of εὐδαιμονία in *EN*. I argued that εὐδαιμονία in EN is best understood as actuality, that there is one account of it in *EN*, and that the need for external goods is due to the lack of self-sufficiency of our human nature. In Chapter 3, I argued that the best reading of εὐδαιμονία in *EN* is based on giving prominence to the main signposts Aristotle uses in I.7 1098a22 ("perimeter of the good") and X.9 1179a35 ("imprint of happiness"). Then, I argued that Aristotle's inquiry on εὐδαιμονία, in its historical diachronic and synchronic development, is the first systematic teleological ethical inquiry in the Greek ancient literature. In Chapter 4, I argued that Aristotle delineates the perimeter of the good by two major criteria: finality and function. The criterion of finality identifies the human good, εὐδιαμονία, as the ultimate, self-sufficient aim which is our actuality. The criterion of function identifies the human good, εὐδαιμονία, as the function of man done well, which is the actuality of our virtuous soul. These two criteria, I argued, delineate the "perimeter of the [human] good."

The main Aristotelian insight into the meaning of εὐδαιμονία is that it is the "actuality of the soul in accordance with virtue" (*EN* I.7 1098a16). To this insight he returns in *EN* X.6 because it can be explored further. Aristotle says that this can be done by studying the "highest virtue" which is the virtue of the highest part of us.

The purpose of this chapter is to offer an interpretation of Aristotle's understanding of εὐδαιμονία in *EN* X.6–8. This will allow me to understand how εὐδαιμονία reaches its completion, which is how we achieve our complete actuality. This chapter has two main sections. In the first section, I will begin by giving my interpretation of how Aristotle continues his ethical inquiry on εὐδαιμονία bringing it to completion in X.6–8. Then, based on this interpretation, I will analyze Bush's dualist interpretation (human versus divine) of εὐδαιμονία here in X.6–8, arguing that εὐδαιμονία reaches its completion in the activity of contemplation (θεωρία). Then, I will present my interpretation of εὐδαιμονία as the actuality of the mind, which is the highest activity a human being can perform. This activity is not only divine, as Bush argues, but both mundane and divine, it can be practiced every day, and it is the most continuous and pleasant a human can have. My conclusion of the first section will be that "imprint of happiness" is Aristotle's way of describing how εὐδαιμονία, delineated by the ultimate aim of man and by the function of man is formed in people's lives and in what degree.

In the second part of the chapter I will argue that εὐδαιμονία, to be formed in someone's life, needs a complete span of life; someone needs a long virtuous life and some modest amount of external goods. I will then debate with Annas about the role of the external goods, arguing that they are needed not because εὐδαιμονία needs them, but because we, as human beings who lack self-sufficiency, need external goods for being able to live. My conclusion to the second part of the chapter will be that εὐδαιμονία is stable enough not to be destroyed by the trials and disasters of life. The "imprint of happiness" is deep, stable, and durable and it cannot be easily dislodged.

5.2 THE COMPLETION OF ARISTOTLE'S INQUIRY ABOUT ΕΥΔΑΙΜΟΝΙΑ IN EN X.6–8

In this section I will argue that Aristotle in *EN* X reaches the last stage of his inquiry on the meaning of εὐδαιμονία. In order to do so, I will identify Aristotle's main sayings which underlie the unity of his account about happiness in *EN*, and how he used them to further his study. Thus, I will present a concise description of Aristotle's own way of summarizing his inquiry through the phrase "imprint of happiness." Then, I will sketch his overall "upward" argument. The aim of this will be described by Aristotle as "complete happiness," which will be my last subsection. I will close this section by arguing that Aristotle keeps his inquiry unitary with the help of criteria of finality and function. The perimeter of the good keeps Aristotle's inquiry about happiness as one account.

5.2.1 "Imprint of happiness"

The last part of Aristotle's inquiry about εὐδαιμονία in *EN* X.6–7 starts by focusing on the unity of his inquiry.[1] By focusing on the unity of his endeavor, he gives the reader a summary of what he had said so far, and this summary is described by him as an "imprint of happiness" (*EN* X.6 1176a30). This summary shows the major features of the "imprint of happiness." It is metaphorical (see 3.1.2) metaphysical language that reviews the stage of his inquiry in the overall movement/change from potentiality to actuality, or from matter to form; the inquiry is near reaching its aim. In this case, in the perimeter of teleology explored in 4.1, I identify his findings as being expressed in metaphysical language.

   According to Aristotle, εὐδαιμονία, as the aim of human life, has to be classed as ἐνέργειαν τινα (*EN* X.6 1176b1). This phrase is usually translated as "some form of activity,"[2] "in the class of activities,"[3] "a sort of activity,"[4] or

---

1. Also, Richardson Lear who says that there are two main reasons for treating the argument about εὐδαιμονία as a unity: 1) there is substantive common ground between Book I and X, and 2) it is the same in *Eudemian Ethics*, Book I, II, and VII, where the focus on virtues and contemplation is peculiar to Aristotle (Richardson Lear, "Happiness," 401).

2. Rackham, *Nicomachean Ethics*.

3. Crisp, *Nicomachean Ethics*.

4. Reeve, *Nicomachean Ethics*.

"a certain activity."[5] The terms "form" or "class" do not appear in Aristotle's text. But what matters for my thesis is how Aristotle brought back, from his initial definition in I.7, an important term to define εὐδαιμονία, and that term is ἐνεργεία. Ἐνεργεία here is identified by Aristotle in some particular way by the term τινα, which is usually translated as "a certain [activity]." I argue that this way of referring to ἐνεργεία with "a certain" activity, confirms my conclusion from 4.2.6, that in Aristotle's philosophy, ἐνεργεία, according to context, has to be understood as "actuality" which is the end result of anyone's potentiality.[6] It is ἐνεργεία understood as "actuality." This reference to εὐδαιμονία as ἐνεργεία makes the connection to the previous definition of εὐδαιμονία in I.7. There, as here, happiness is described as "activity/actuality" [ἐνεργεία].[7]

This activity is an activity desired for what it is in itself (*EN* X.6 1177a2), an activity that has everything, that is self-sufficient (*EN* X.6 1176b5). It is not an activity serving as a means to something else, but it is an end itself (*EN* X.6 1176b7). As in I.7, this activity is virtuous (*EN* X.6 1176a10). Aristotle's summary from X.6 confirms my overall metaphysical formative interpretation of εὐδαιμονία because he says that everything so far in *EN* was a discussion about happiness and virtue in their various "forms" [τύποις] (*EN* X.9 1179a35). As I argued in 3.1.2, τύπος as "imprint" is a main term that defines Aristotle's approach to εὐδαιμονία as an educational formative process. Thus, Aristotle's study intended to leave an imprint of happiness in people's lives, it is a transformative study/endeavor.

Thus, I understand the "imprint" of happiness as a metaphysical educational metaphor. As I argued in 3.1.2, a metaphor, according to Aristotle, is "the application of an alien name by transference" (*Poetics* 3.21).[8] Here in *EN* X.6, Aristotle "transfers" the alien name of "the mark of the blow" [τύπος] to an unexpected context, which is that of εὐδαιμονία. According to Aristotle, a good metaphor is "the mark of genius, for to make good metaphors implies an eye for resemblances" (*Poetics* 3.21).[9] As a result of

5. Bartlett, and Collins, *Nicomachean Ethics*.

6. Unlike Baracchi who explains, succinctly, ἐνεργεία in functional terms as 'being-at-work.' There is no detailed study on ἐνεργεία in her chapter on 'Happiness' but the focus is on 'inseparability of ends and means' and ἐνεργεία is the task at work: 'being-at-work well is the end' (Baracchi, *Ethics*, 96).

7. Against Van Cleemput who argues for 'one [happy] life, but two different activities' (Van Cleemput, "Happiness," 95).

8. Fyfe, *Poetics*.

9. Fyfe, *Poetics*.

the blow, something is formed, an imprint, and it is this resemblance Aristotle observes between τύπος and εὐδαιμονία: the general notion of form. Because a form is obtained, I argue, that this a metaphysical educational/formative metaphor. It points to the climax of Aristotle's worldview, people moving from their potentiality to actuality, or from matter to form. Thus, εὐδαιμονία as some kind of ἐνεργεία (as actuality) is to be seen as a "form" obtained by "a blow." This is how his teleological metaphysical ethics is presented and applied. Thus, is this chapter I will argue that this "imprint of happiness" reaches it completion in the activity/actuality of contemplation [θεωρία], and this completion is the teleological metaphysical climax of the whole inquiry in Aristotelian political science. This is how a "blow" achieves its "form."

5.2.2 Advancing upward

After the review of the "imprint of happiness" (EN X.6 1176a31–1177a10) is done, Aristotle makes an important move in advancing his inquiry. He says: "if happiness consists in activity in accordance with virtue, it is reasonable that it should be the activity in accordance with the highest virtue; and this will be the virtue of the best part of us" (EN X.7 1177a12). So, he builds on his previous findings and advances upwards:[10] now he focuses on the "highest virtue" of ἐνεργεία. That is why what he does in X.6 is not a new account of happiness, but a completion of the previous one, from Books I and II.

This upward inquiry has a challenge: the best part of us is the intellect, and the intellect, according to Aristotle, is divine (EN X.7 1177b30); and this makes it superior to the human side of our composite nature. The way Aristotle keeps his inquiry together is by saying that these two lives, "the life of the intellect" and "the life of moral virtue" are two stages/degrees available to humans (EN X.8 1178a10). He will continue to apply the main criterion of the "function of man" as this is said explicitly in EN X.7 1178a7: "that which is best and most pleasant for each creature is that which is proper to the nature of each." This underlines the unity of his inquiry but here it reaches the ultimate climax.

---

10. Against Shields who argues that in EN Aristotle seems to move from an encompassing understanding of the human good to a narrow understanding of it consisting in contemplation. These two conceptions of the good are not coherent (Shields, *Aristotle*, 341).

Thus, in *EN* X.6–8, Aristotle's inquiry on the good of man is reaching its end. This "reaching its end" language has to be interpreted in the larger Aristotelian metaphysical framework in which a thing is moved from matter to form, or from potentiality to actuality. As I argued in 4.1.2, the "pure actuality," in Aristotle's metaphysics, is the unmoved mover, god. When someone gets closer in achieving the actuality of his or her potentiality, his or her life is blessed "in so far as it contains some likeness to the divine activity" (*EN* X.8 1178b27).[11] In this metaphysical framework I interpret the phrase "complete happiness" (*EN* X.7 1177a17, 10.8 1178b7) as happiness reaching its completion as I will explain in the following subsection.

5.2.3 Complete happiness

Aristotle is very careful not to use the phrase "secondary happiness" as some scholars do.[12] "Secondary happiness" is usually understood by these scholars as referring to a distinct kind of life, a virtuous life distinct from a divine life. They work with this distinction between "virtuous human life" and "divine life." I argue that Aristotle speaks here about different stages in people's lives as they strive towards "complete happiness." It is like a singer who, through practice and competition, finally achieves his/her goal of winning a major award or being able to interpret well a major work of music. S/he achieved mastery in that field of work. Aristotle's exact words in *EN* X.8 1078a10 are: "in a secondary degree, on the other hand, that according to the other virtue" [Δευτέρος δ᾽ ὁ κατὰ τὴν ἄλλην ἀρετήν]. The immediate context of *EN* X.7 1078a9 speaks about the "life that is happiest," not a "different happy life." The meaning of δευτέρος in *EN* X.8 1078a10 is related to a *degree*, not to a distinct kind of life. Aristotle's "happiness as the actuality of the soul according to virtue" is not a "secondary happiness" but a stage secondary to last, that can be completed in "complete happiness."

As I argued in 4.2.6, happiness is the activity according virtue (this is "the other virtue" in X.8 1078a10).[13] This was the result of his inquiry up

11. Long says that "the gods are the paradigms of happiness" (Long, "Eudaimonia," 111; see also Kraut, *Human Good*, 325). There is a passing mention about the larger metaphysical framework by Roochnik when he says that 'theoretical activity actualizes what is most divine in us' (Roochnik, "*Theoria*," 69, but he does not elaborate as his work is only a prolegomenon to a study of θεωρία.

12. See Hardie, "Final Good," 279, 282; Hardie, "Best Life," 48; Shea, "Happiness," 83; Majithia, "Good Life," 8; Van Cleemput, "Happiness," 131; Kraut, *Human Good*, 322, 323.

13. Ross, *Nicomachean Ethics*.

to *EN* X.6 and, now he develops his thesis by exploring it according to "the highest virtue." This shows that Aristotle works with a hierarchical structure of virtues that allows him to go higher in his inquiry; the higher the part of us, the higher its virtue. Also, the concept of τέλος/aim/end prompts him to go all the way up to the end with his inquiry. This is how continuity with the initial definition of εὐδαιμονία (activity/actuality of the soul according to virtue) and its completion (now Aristotle speaks about "complete happiness"), has to be understood: the activity according to (the other) virtue, and the activity according to highest virtue. There is continuity between "activity/actuality of the soul according to virtue" and the "activity/actuality in accordance with the highest virtue," which is the virtue of "the best part of us." Thus, there are not two kinds of happiness, one that is "primary" and the other that is "secondary"; Aristotle does not have two accounts of εὐδαιμονία, but one[14] (see my analysis of the debate in 2.2.2). In Aristotle there is "happiness" and "*complete* happiness" or the good of man and the good of man *reaching its end*.[15] Not everyone reaches the actuality of his or her potentiality, but only those who are living/working according to their highest virtue.[16] Thus, the perimeter of τέλος reaches its maximum area and the imprint of εὐδαιμονία is formed. This is how actuality is reached by humans.

So, in this section I argued that Aristotle's inquiry about happiness, started in Book I and II, is reaching its completion in Book X.6. Accordingly, εὐδαιμονία continues to be, for Aristotle in *EN*, the actuality, but now he explores this by focusing on the highest virtue, which is the virtue of the highest part of us, the intellect. Because Aristotle continues to understand εὐδαιμονία as ἐνεργεία the metaphysical aspect is still present and is further explored. The intellect is the divine part of us and that is why its actuality will be the closest we can get to the "pure actuality" which is god. The activity of the intellect, contemplation, resembles the activity of the gods. This is "complete happiness," εὐδαιμονία reaching its completion.

14. Against Curzer who says that the criteria used by Aristotle's inquiry about εὐδαιμονία in *EN* X.6–8 and I.7 are very different (Curzer, "Criteria," 422). Richardson Lear argues for one account of εὐδαιμονία in *EN* and says that the moral action 'approximates' contemplation (Richardson Lear, *Happy Lives*, 177).

15. Also, Majithia who argues that 'the good life for the virtuous man is the life of practical virtue ending in contemplation' (Majithia, "Good Life," 8).

16. Also, Pakaluk who says that 'happiness in Aristotelian scheme is meant to be an ideal not a catch-all for people' (Pakaluk, *Nicomachean Ethics*, 322).

5.3 BUSH ON DIVINE AND HUMAN HAPPINESS

In this next section I debate with Bush because he has argued for an understanding of "complete happiness" that is not developed according with the classic debate of "inclusive/dominant" interpretations of εὐδαιμονία, and because he is willing to explore the divine aspect of Aristotle's inquiry, as I do. In today's secular research climate this is rare. I will present the details of his argument about the difference between human and divine happiness, and then, I will present my objections to his interpretation. I will argue that there are strong factors that point towards one account of εὐδαιμονία, not two, as Bush interprets *EN* X.6–8. Also, I will argue that εὐδαιμονία is achievable, potentially, for everyone in the city willing to form the life according to the highest virtue; θεώρια is not an exclusive divine activity but encompasses a variety of activities, both mundane and divine.

Bush starts his inquiry by enunciating the problem faced by every interpreter of *EN* X.6–8: if happiness is found in the "excellent philosophical contemplation about the loftiest questions" what about "the status of morally virtuous activity and about the relation between that activity and contemplation?"[17] He, then, makes an important observation, which I have mentioned several times so far in my project (see 2.1 and 2.2.2): the interpreters have to settle "whether happiness is a monistic good [. . .], or an inclusive good. How one answers this question to a large degree determines one's conclusion about the relation between morally virtuous activity and contemplation."[18] Bush sees, as I do, that the monistic/inclusive debate dominates the interpretation of εὐδαιμονία in almost all aspects. Bush favors the monistic interpretation, but he finds it "ultimately untenable,"[19] and departs from it by arguing for a "dualistic"[20] interpretation of εὐδαιμονία.

Arguing against the monistic interpretation, Bush says that:

> if the human good is philosophical contemplation, and other goods are choiceworthy when chosen for the sake of contemplation, what status does that leave for morally virtuous activity? It would be counter-intuitive to the point of implausibility to hold that acts of courage and justice are not intrinsically valuable,

---

17. Bush, "Happiness," 49.
18. Bush, "Happiness," 50.
19. Bush, "Happiness," 51.
20. Bush, "Happiness," 51.

but only have value when chosen for the sake of philosophical contemplation.[21]

Bush considers that the monistic interpreters (he debates with Richardson Lear and Cooper) have not yet given "an explanation of how Aristotle can regard the life of morally virtuous activity as happy."[22] Bush is highly critical and here are his sharpest objections against the dominant/monistic interpretation:

> If only the activity of contemplation is happiness, how could a life devoid of contemplation (as all agree the political life is) be considered happy, even in a secondary, deficient sense?
> . . . So, the monist's insistence that a person's life can attain the state of happiness without containing the activity of happiness should give us pause.[23]

This is the harsh rejection by Bush of the monistic/intellectualist interpretation of εὐδαιμονία.

Bush argues for a reading that makes a clear distinction between the "complete happiness as the divine good" (which is not a human good) and "the human good [which] is the activity that is characteristically human: morally virtuous activity."[24] According to Bush, contemplation does not qualify as a human good because it is a divine good.[25] Thus, Bush applies the argument of the "function of man" to say that there is a clear dualism in Aristotle's inquiry on εὐδαιμονία. Bush says that there is "a distinction between the peculiar human good and the highest good that human can obtain."[26] This distinction is the basis of Bush's position. For him, the human good is the activity that is virtuous, but contemplation is a divine good.[27] What is peculiar to human beings is their "ability to conform [their] activities to reason, and the element that 'itself thinks' is the soul."[28]

Based on this point, Bush focuses on the distinctions used by Aristotle to speak about the divine aspect of man. He says that when a person

21. Bush, "Happiness," 52.

22. Bush, "Happiness," 53.

23. Bush, "Happiness," 53, 59.

24. Bush, "Happiness," 51.

25. Bush, "Happiness," 51.

26. Bush, "Happiness," 62.

27. Bush, "Happiness," 62.

28. Bush, "Happiness," 63.

lives his/her life in accordance with intelligence (which is divine), his/her life is divine.[29] According to Bush, what that person contemplates is also divine.[30] Thus, contemplation is an activity that gods do. Because of this it cannot be an activity peculiar to us, humans.[31] Based on these distinctions Bush states that "contemplation is not a human good, and so not the highest human good."[32]

To consolidate this dualistic reading, Bush explores the differences between the definitions of εὐδαιμονία given by Aristotle in I.7 and in X.7. According to Bush, in *EN* I.7 Aristotle gives a definition of the human good, whereas in X.7 he does not. This is so because, Bush says, there is no mention of the human good or of the soul in *EN* X.7.[33] There are these differences in what Aristotle says, according to Bush, because Aristotle works with some of the same criteria for identifying the human good in I.7 to identify the divine good in X.7. Aristotle also says, according to Bush, that the contemplation, the divine good, can be reached by humans.[34] Because of this distinction, Bush says that people should seek this happiness related to contemplation, the divine good; this happiness is better than the human happiness which is the activity according to virtue.[35]

I criticize the "dualistic" reading proposed by Bush at the following three major points: 1) his general criticism against the monistic interpretation of εὐδαιμονία, 2) his sharp distinction between "complete happiness" and the "human good," and 3) his interpretation of "complete happiness" a divine good.

My first objection is concerning his general criticism against the dominant/monistic interpretation. Even if I do not read *EN* following the monistic/inclusive debates (see my proposal for a "new reading" in 3.1.1 and 3.1.2), I consider Bush's main line of attack to fail. His objection is about the human good. Which is it? Philosophical contemplation or morally virtuous activity? What is the status of virtuous activities if we choose everything for the sake of contemplation?[36] This criticism fails because it does not re-

29. Bush, "Happiness," 64.

30. Bush, "Happiness," 64.

31. Bush, "Happiness," 65.

32. Bush, "Happiness," 65.

33. Bush, "Happiness," 67.

34. Bush, "Happiness," 67.

35. Bush, "Happiness," 68.

36. Bush, "Happiness," 52.

flect what Aristotle does in his overall inquiry: there is continuity between the good of man as happiness (activity/actuality of the soul according to virtue) and complete happiness (activity/actuality according to the highest virtue). The "imprint of happiness" [εὐδαιμονίας τύπῳ] provided by Aristotle in *EN* X.6 1176a30–1177a10 as the main metaphysical educational metaphor shows the results of his inquiry up to this point. The continuity of Aristotle's inquiry between these two sections (Books I, II and Book X.6) is explained above. And from there (*EN* X.6) he continues focusing on the "activity in accordance with [. . .] the highest virtue" (*EN* X.7 1177a12). This is a continuation of his inquiry into the area of virtues, and, because Aristotle works with a hierarchical understanding of virtues, in the end it is reasonable that he will focus on the "highest virtue."

To make a sharp distinction between "philosophical contemplation" and "morally virtuous activity" as Bush does in *EN* is a mistake.[37] The "philosophical contemplation" is the main aim of Aristotle's inquiry on the "highest virtue." Aristotle did not change the line of his inquiry (switching from the human good to the divine good, as Bush says), but he brings his inquiry to its teleological completion following his metaphysical framework of moving from potentiality to actuality. The "moral virtuous activity" reaches its final end/aim in the "activity according to the highest virtue." This is Aristotle main point in *EN* X.7, that because εὐδαιμονία is activity according to virtue, "it is reasonable that it should be" the activity according to the highest virtue. This is how there is continuity and upward movement in Aristotle's inquiry. All virtuous acts have value when they are chosen for the sake of happiness that reaches its completeness, and that is the "activity according to the highest virtue." I do not know how Richardson Lear or Cooper answer[38] to the objections brought by Bush against them, but this is my answer to Bush. It is an answer based on Aristotelian metaphysical teleological ethics.

My second objection is against Bush's sharp distinction between "complete happiness" and the "human good." The "human good," according to Bush, is the "moral virtuous activity," and the "complete happiness" is a "divine good." Bush says that Aristotle does not use the phrase "human good" in *EN* X.6–8 when he discuses the "complete happiness." It is true

37. Bush, "Happiness," 62, 65.

38. Bush's article (2008) was published after Richardson Lear, *Happy Lives* and Cooper, *Knowledge*. Richardson Lear does not offer an answer in her later publication: Richardson Lear, "Happiness."

that Aristotle does not use the phrase "human good" in this part of the *EN* X, but this does not mean that "the complete happiness" is not "the human good." I argue this based on *EN* X.9 1179a34-b7. There, Aristotle gives the reader the result of his entire inquiry: it has been a discussion about the "imprint [of] happiness and virtue in its various forms" and this investigation is not complete until "we must endeavor to possess and to practice it, or in some other manner actually ourselves to become good." Humans become good when they "carry out [their] theories in action" (*EN* X.9 1179b2). The possibility and the need to transfer theory into practice shows that there is continuity between the "complete happiness" as the ultimate teleological end, and the "human good." The "complete happiness" is not a distinct kind of good, namely a "divine good" in contrast to a "human good," but the human good reaching its aim, its actuality.

My third objection is against Bush's seeing the complete happiness as a divine good. Bush argues for this understanding based on the function argument (*EN* I.7). Bush says that, because the intellect is divine, what we contemplate is divine, and contemplation is peculiar to the gods.[39]

The fact is that Aristotle does not use these phrases: "divine good" and "highest human good." Instead he uses the phrases "divine activity" (*EN* X.8. 1178b20), "highest virtue" (*EN* X.7 1177a13), and "highest form of activity" (*EN* X.7 1177a20) to speak about contemplation [θεωρία]. Bush's phrases are a strong effort to create a sharp distinction in Aristotle's inquiry between human and divine goods. Bush says that in *EN* X.6-8 Aristotle does not use the phrase "human good," which is true; and because of this fact that Aristotle does not use the phrase "human good" in *EN* X.6-8, Bush argues that "complete happiness" is not a "human good." Then, Bush uses the phrases "divine good" and "highest human good," not used by Aristotle, to talk about "complete happiness."

Thus, Bush tries to have it both ways: on the one hand he exploits the fact that the phrase "human good" is not used to describe "complete happiness" in X.6-9, and on the other hand, he uses the phrase "divine good" (not used by Aristotle in X.6-9) to describe "complete happiness." The fact that Aristotle did not use the phrase "human good" to describe "complete happiness" is used to argue that "complete happiness" is not a "human good," and then, he creates a phrase (the highest divine good) to describe the meaning of "complete happiness." In other words, the fact that

39. Bush, "Happiness," 64.

Aristotle does not describe "complete happiness" as a human good, gives an opportunity to Bush to describe it as he wants, as the "highest divine good."

I argue that the "complete happiness" of humans is not a "divine good," as Bush says, but the happiness which reaches its actuality or its form ("imprint of happiness"). In this ultimate respect of arriving at its actuality, happiness [εὐδαιμονία] is contemplation [θεωρία]. The continuity in Aristotle's inquiry can be seen by observing how the "function argument" is developed.[40] Aristotle, in *EN* I.7, defines the function of man in terms of "a certain form of life." This "form" of life takes place when a human being exercises his or her faculties of the soul. The function of a good human being is to practice these activities well (*EN* I.7 1098a14). Based on these premises, Aristotle argues that the good of man is the activity/actuality of the soul in accordance with the best and most perfect virtues (*EN* I.7 1098a15). This understanding of the "function of man" is reiterated in *EN* X.7 1178a5 as: "that which is best and most pleasant for each creature is that which is proper to the nature of each."

Bush builds his argument that "complete happiness" is not a "human good" but a "divine good" based on the fact that contemplation is not "peculiar to man" but to gods. The function argument, as it is used in *EN* I.7 and X.7, shows that what is "peculiar" to man is but the start, and it has to go to what is the "best part of us." What is "peculiar" to man is not something that remains/stays the same, but something that develops, and this development has to be understood in the larger metaphysical teleological framework. What I say is that a man should become a good man. Thus, what is "peculiar" to him should become the starting point for what is best and most perfect to/for him. Thus, we have "the active exercise of his soul's faculties according to the best and most perfect virtue" (*EN* I.7 1098a18) and then "the activity according to the highest virtue" (*EN* X.7 1117a14). This "highest virtue" is the virtue of the "best part of us," which is the intellect. The potentiality of man to reach his/her actuality is possible because of the intellect. And the actuality or form in the Aristotelian teleological metaphysics is understood in terms of divinity. I will explore these aspects later in section 5.3.

In conclusion, in this section I argued that Bush's sharp distinction between "complete happiness" and the "human good," does not find strong support in Aristotle's text of *EN* X.6, and that "complete happiness" is not

---

40. See also Prichard who says that Aristotle bases his argument about happiness as contemplation "on the idea that man has a function" (Prichard, "ἀγαθόν," 37).

the "divine good." Aristotle does not use the important phrase "complete happiness" is such a way. My position is that Aristotle searches for a way in which his previous definition of εὐδαιμονία from I.7 as the "activity of the soul according to virtue" can be explored further in the larger perimeter of the good, where the two main criteria of finality and function guide him towards actuality, the complete happiness.

So far, in this chapter, I have argued that Aristotle, in *EN* X.6–8, brings to completion his inquiry into the meaning of εὐδαιμονία; he started his study about εὐδαιμονία in Books I and II. I argued that there is common space between "virtuous activity" and "contemplation" as both of them are about the actuality of human beings. It is not that the "virtuous activity" is inferior, and that "contemplation" is superior. No. The first one constitutes actuality at the overall level of the soul and there are people who experience it and live a happy life, and the second one constitutes actuality at the focused level of intellect (which is, according to Aristotle, an element of the soul) and there are people who experience it and live a happy life. But, we should not forget, both of them are virtuous lives. The fact is that, for Aristotle in *EN*, εὐδαιμονία is ἐνεργεία, happiness is actuality, happiness has to be understood as the ultimate aim of a movement, a movement from potentiality to actuality. So the difference between virtuous activity and contemplation is that contemplation is the upper end of this movement, and the common ground is that both of them are activities of the soul and intellect. The activity of contemplation is the actuality of the intellect. In this way the highest part of us reaches its best, which is its actuality. That is complete happiness. It is like entering the process of education in philosophy with the purpose of becoming a college professor. Some will manage to reach the position of adjunct professors (Community/Junior College level) and others tenured professors (College, University level). Both of these groups are virtuous people and have reached their actuality but the difference between them is that the second group managed to go further in the pursuit for the highest position possible, that of university professor.

5.4 ACTIVITY IN ACCORDANCE WITH THE HIGHEST VIRTUE: ΘΕΩΡΙΑ

In this section I will study the last segment of Aristotle's inquiry: ἐνεργεία in accordance with the highest virtue. The highest virtue is the virtue of the highest part of us, which is the intellect [νοῦς]. First, I will explain how we need to understand the intellect as an element of the soul, and, second, how we need to understand contemplation [θεώρια] both as "study" and "contemplation." I will argue that the ultimate teleological end of man is the actuality [ἐνέργεια] of the mind/intellect [νοῦς], and because the νοῦς, according to Aristotle, is an element of every human soul, this actuality is a possibility for every human being. This section is needed because its topic is Aristotle's topic at the climax of his investigation.

5.4.1 Intellect as an element of the soul

In this subsection I will study the intellect, the highest part of us. I will focus my investigation by giving an overview of how intellect, as the highest part of us, is understood by Aristotle in *EN*, then, what is its role as an element of every human soul, and in the end what does it mean that for Aristotle the intellect is divine. I will argue that for Aristotle, in his ethical inquiry, the intellect is the main factor of the soul which constitutes the potentiality which can lead to achieving of actuality in every human life.

In *EN* X. 6–8, Aristotle continues to inquiry into the area of virtues by focusing on the "highest" [κράτιστη] [virtue]; Aristotle searches for the "most excellent" virtue. The way he searches for the most excellent virtue is by exploring it according to the "function" framework. For him the "most excellent" virtue is the virtue of the "best part" [ἄριστος] of us. This is the virtue "proper to it" (*EN* X.7 1177a14). Aristotle identifies the "best part of us" as the part that "rules and leads us by nature." That part "has cognizance of what is noble and divine" (*EN* X.7 1177a15). And this is the mind/intellect [νοῦς].

Thus, the factors of ruling, leading, and knowing of the noble and divine are the factors used by Aristotle to identify what is best [ἄριστος]. Also "the best" [ἄριστος], which is the mind/intellect [νοῦς] is "divine" [θεῖον] (*EN* X.7 1177a15). This is the part of us humans that ultimately helps to reach the aim of our potentiality, which is happiness, our actuality. Because the mind [νοῦς] is divine we are able to reach our actuality; god, according to Aristotle, is the pure actuality. The ἐνέργεια of the mind, which is a human activity, is "the greatest source of happiness" (*EN* X.8 1178b25). To understand better what Aristotle says about νοῦς in *EN* X.6–8, I need to explore his view on it, as he speaks about it in *EN*.

For Aristotle, νοῦς is found in the soul. In the soul, according to Aristotle, there are three elements: intellect [νοῦς], sensation, and desire.

Through them a human being gains control upon his/her actions and attains truth (*EN* VI.2 1139a19). Aristotle understands humans as creatures of action, and as such, they are a compound of "desire and intellect" [νοῦς] (*EN* VI.2 1139b5). The human mind attains truth with the help of several qualities: "technical skill, scientific knowledge, prudence, wisdom, and intelligence" [τέχνη ἐπιστήμη φρόνησις σοφία νοῦς] (*EN* VI.3 1139b16). From these qualities only, the mind [νοῦς] is the quality through which humans can apprehend the "first principles" (*EN* VI.3 1139b16).

Also, Aristotle understands wisdom [σοφία] as a combination of mind [νοῦς] and knowledge [ἐπιστήμη]. This knowledge, according to Aristotle, is the knowledge of the "most exalted objects" (*EN* VI.7 1141a20). Through wisdom we have knowledge and intelligence of the "things of the most exalted nature" (*EN* VI.7 1141b3). Our intelligence [νοῦς] has the ability to "apprehend definitions" (*EN* VI.8 1142a25; see the extended analysis about this in *EN* VI.11 1143a25-b15). This focus on wisdom (mind and knowledge) and the most exalted things will be resurfacing in *EN* X.8, where the philosopher as a wise man is the happiest person, and this person is a person who reaches his/her actuality. I will explore it further below.

In the good man, the intellect [νοῦς] "always chooses for itself that which is best." A good man obeys his intellect (*EN* IX.8 1169a18), and together with virtue [ἀρετή], the intellect/mind [νοῦς] is the "source of man's higher activities" (*EN* X.6 1176b19). This is what Aristotle says in *EN* about the intellect [νοῦς] before *EN* X.7. An informed interpretation of the intellect [νοῦς] in X.7 needs to take these aspects into consideration. These details about the νοῦς are rarely mentioned and integrated by scholars (for example, Bush 2008, Nagel 1972, Hardie 1979 do not explore it).

So, according to Aristotle, νοῦς is part of every human soul, not only some, and the νοῦς is the factor that makes the reaching of actuality possible for every human being. The soul is the main element of continuity in his inquiry between what was said before *EN* X.7 and after that. In *EN* I.7 1098a16 Aristotle's conclusion is that "the good of man is the active exercise of his soul's faculties in conformity with excellence." Now in *EN* X.7-8 he explores the νοῦς as one of the elements in the soul, because this element has two main features: it rules and leads us and knows what is noble and divine (*EN* X.7 1177a12). Aristotle has a comprehensive way of expressing this in *EN* VI.11 1143b10: "intelligence is both beginning and end" [ἀρχὴ καὶ τέλος νοῦς], which means that "ultimates as well as primary are grasped by intelligence" [τῶν πρώτων ὅρων καὶ τῶν ἐσχάτων νοῦς ἐστὶ] (*EN* VI.11

1143b1). These exact quotes are very important because they show how important νοῦς is for Aristotle in relation to the first principles (the beginning) and the ultimate purpose of everything. They are apprehended by the νοῦς. Because of νοῦς this movement towards the ultimate aim [τέλος] is possible.

Also, Aristotle says that "intellect is divine" [θεῖον ὁ νοῦς] (EN X.7 1177b30). This fact is explored by Aristotle by way of a comparison between a life at "the human level" [κατ' ἄνθρωπον] (EN X.7 1177b27) and the "higher life" [βίος κρείττων] (EN X.7 1177b27). This higher life is possible for a human because of the νοῦς, which is divine and superior. Thus, the life of the νοῦς is divine when it is compared with human life (EN X.7 1177b34). Aristotle advises humanity to make sure that they live their lives in accordance with their intellect which is the highest part in them (EN X.7 1177b34). He advises them to keep their intellect in the best condition, and to cultivate it by pursuing rational intellectual activities (EN X.8 1179a24). These actions of "pursuing," "cultivating," and "preserving" the intellect are ways in which every human should relate to his/her νοῦς. According to Aristotle the wise man practices these actions (EN X.8 1179a30). According to him, the wise man is "naturally" the happiest [εὐδαιμονέστατον] person and s/he is most loved by the gods (EN X.8 1179a32). This is the last point in Aristotle's inquiry.

This last point about actuality/activity according to the highest virtue has to be seen not as a distinct stage but as the potential aim for everyone; the νοῦς is the most powerful and valuable part a person has (EN X.7 1178a1), and it has the ability to apprehend the first principles and the most exalted things in nature. The reference to "first principles" and the "most exalted things" has to be understood in the larger metaphysical Aristotelian framework. I explored it in 4.1.2. As I argued there, Meth XII is the relevant text of Aristotle for understanding his inquiry [θεωρία] on οὐσία [substance]. Studying/contemplating the "substance" gives Aristotle the occasion to understand its principles, elements, and causes. This activity/actuality of νοῦς, contemplation, makes it possible. Ultimately, in the Aristotelian framework, the most exalted item to contemplate is the immovable substance, the unmoved mover, god, the pure actuality. Thus, with the help of νοῦς, the good/virtuous person can practice "higher activities."

Thus, the activity/actuality of "the best part of us" in "accordance with virtue proper to it that will constitute perfect happiness" (EN X.7 1177a17). But what is this activity proper to the "best part" of us? I will present my answer in the next subsection.

5.4.2 Θεωρία as study and contemplation

In this subsection I will study θεωρία as the ultimate activity of man, as presented by Aristotle. I will begin by arguing that contemplation is the final point of the function argument of Aristotle in *EN*, then, I will provide an overview of how θεωρία is used by Aristotle in *EN*. I will argue that teleology is the best context to interpret θεωρία in *EN*, and, then, based on this teleological interpretation of θεωρία, I will answer various questions about θεωρία and virtuous actions. I will argue that θεωρία is *both* a human *and* a divine activity, and, according to Aristotle, it is *both* study *and* admiration/beholding. Because θεωρία is an activity of the intellect, every human being can practice it in various measures and ways. That is why θεωρία is available to anyone. It is a possibility that can reach actuality in every human life.

So what is the activity of the highest part of us? Aristotle's answer is this: contemplation [θεωρία], which is the activity of the mind/intellect [νοῦς]. When the intellect [νοῦς] acts at its best, that is when it "rules and leads us" and "has cognizance of what is noble and divine" (*EN* X.7 1177a15) it contemplates. When the human mind is in control of our lives and we are guided by it, when we discern what has quality and what is divine, we contemplate. This is what constitutes contemplation. This is θεωρία, the activity of contemplation, which "constitutes perfect happiness." This is how Aristotle's inquiry explores further the definition of happiness as the "activity of the soul in accordance with virtue": it goes specifically into the soul and identifies νοῦς as the "best part of us" and then, focuses on the virtue of the νοῦς. This is how he arrives at θεωρία.

Εὐδαιμονία as an "activity of the soul according to excellence" reaches its ultimate end/expression in contemplation [θεωρία], the "highest form of activity" [κρατίστη. . . ἡ ἐνέργεια] (*EN* X.7 1177a20). Contemplation is the "highest form of activity" because it is the activity of the intellect which is the "highest thing in us," and because the intellect deals with the "highest things" that a human being can know (*EN* X.7 1177a22). Because contemplation is the highest form of activity, it is the ultimate actuality for humans. This is how the function argument reaches its ultimate possibility: what is proper to the highest part of us, the intellect [νοῦς], is contemplation [θεωρία], and contemplation focuses on the things noble and divine. Aristotle confirms this by making reference to the animals, which have no share in happiness. The animals are devoid of it because they do not have the ability to contemplate (*EN* X.8 1178b28). If a "class of beings" possesses inherently the ability of contemplation it "enjoys happiness," otherwise happiness is not possible. Aristotle says that "happiness is co-extensive in its range with contemplation" (EN X.8 1178b29).

These important and specific features of contemplation [θεωρία] do not jeopardize Aristotle's inquiry about εὐδαιμονία. The "results reached so far" (EN X.7 1177a18) are in agreement with it, and here are Aristotle's points: contemplation as an activity is our highest and most continuous one, it is an activity that gives us pleasure, it is the most self-sufficient, and we love it for what it is. In other words, we as humans are able to contemplate or reflect by ourselves and more continuously, and our search for wisdom gives us pleasure, and the contemplation in itself is the ultimate result/actuality. These insights are presented extensively in EN X.7 1177a18–b1 and they explore the agreement between this last stage of contemplation [θεωρία] and the previous ones of finality [τελός] and function [ἔργον]. Thus, the activity of contemplation, as the activity of the highest virtue, is the function argument reaching its ultimate end.

Now, for a better understanding of θεωρία, I need to enlarge the area of investigation beyond EN X.6–8; that is why I need to bring in other important affirmations of Aristotle from EN. I criticized Bush for his sharp distinction between "divine happiness" and "human happiness." Bush argues for this distinction based on his understanding of θεωρία as being mainly a divine activity. That is why the question I have to test is this: Is θεωρία mainly a divine activity in EN and Aristotle's writings in general? David Roockhnik[41] says no. He argues for both a "mundane" and "divine" meaning of θεωρία. Roochnik's study does not engage with the issues of Aristotle's inquiry in EN about εὐδαιμονία; his study is only a philological "prolegomena" on θεωρία.

Θεωρία is a divine activity. But this is not the best and the only way Aristotle understands it. If θεωρία is only a divine activity, the Aristotelian political science is in danger of not reaching its ultimate end, "the complete happiness." There are sayings of Aristotle in EN that point also towards a mundane meaning. He says that the whole project of EN is a θεωρία: "as then our present study [θεωρίας], unlike the other branches of philosophy, has a practical aim" (EN II.2 1103b26). The same meaning is in EN VII.3 1146b13, where Aristotle uses θεωρία for his "study."[42] In EN IV.2 Aristotle speaks about the achievements of the "magnificent man." These honored and great achievements of him are admired by others, and this process

41. Roochnik, "Theoria."
42. Irwin, Nicomachean Ethics.

of beholding, or contemplation of, these achievements is described by Aristotle with the term θεωρία (*EN* IV.2 1122b18).[43] This reference from *EN* IV.2 brings together the terms achievements/works [ἔργον] and contemplation [θεωρία]. For Aristotle, the most honored work/function is admirable to behold. "Beholding" something admirable is what θεωρία is in this text. Then, in *EN* X.4 1174b22 Aristotle speaks about the pleasure given by the activity of study.[44] Perhaps the whole project of *EN* gave Aristotle this pleasure too. It is clear then, in these references from *EN* IV.2 and X.4, that Aristotle understands θεώρια as a very human activity, the activity of study and beholding.

These two have to be kept together, inquiry and admiration. Thus, before *EN* X.7–8 these are the ways in which Aristotle speaks about θεωρία, and it is an activity proper to man. I argue that the better interpretation of θεωρία is one that is able to integrate the entire inquiry of *EN*,[45] which means that θεώρια in *EN* is both human and divine activity.[46]

5.4.2.1 Θεωρία *and teleology*

We need to remember that Aristotle's inquiry about εὐδαιμονία is an inquiry that has to be read teleologically. In this project, I argue that Aristotle, in *EN*, works with two major metaphors—"perimeter" and "imprint"—to present his understanding of εὐδαιμονία. For Aristotle, the perimeter of teleology is an ever-expanding one because of the movement towards actuality. The highest part of us, the νοῦς, being shared by every human, and being divine, is the factor that helps us to achieve our actuality, which is becoming more like the gods. Being more like the gods means being engaged in the activity of contemplation as they are. That is why I argue that Aristotle's presentation of θεώρια in *EN* is better read in this teleological perspective, and not in a "dualistic" way, as Bush argues.

Then, I argue that in this "perimeter" an imprint is "blown"/formed, and this "imprint" is the imprint of the highest activity/actuality proper to

43. Ross, *Nicomachean Ethics*.

44. Irwin, *Nicomachean Ethics*.

45. Unlike Burger who understands contemplation as being an "essentially solitary activity" (Burger, *Nicomachean Ethics*, 25).

46. See also Curzer who says that "contemplation is not limited to intense concentration upon esoteric objects, but also includes concentration and reflection upon the ordinary affairs of human life" (Curzer, *Virtues*, 424).

the intellect, the highest part of us. Thus, I argue that to study about and to contemplate what is noble and divine is the ultimate actuality, it is the complete εὐδαιμονία. In this way the whole inquiry is kept together, and not split as Bush says, and these two metaphysical educational metaphors of "perimeter" and "imprint" are the major factors in it.

5.4.2.2 Θεωρία and virtuous actions

Every study on εὐδαιμονία needs to address the relationship between contemplation and virtuous actions. In this subsection I will study two important questions in this regard. The first is about the meaning of the saying from *EN* X.8 1178a9 about the moral virtue being happy in a secondary degree, and the second concerns the classic criticism against every dominant or monist interpretation of εὐδαιμονία as concerning the moral status of virtuous action. I will argue that the "secondary degree" in relation to virtuous actions refers to the second-to-last stage in the movement towards complete happiness. And in relation to the moral status of virtuous action, I will argue that moral, virtuous activity reaches its completion in contemplation.

Now, if this teleological-unitary reading of εὐδαιμονία as θεώρια is a better interpretation, how do I explain the difficult affirmation from *EN* X.8 1178a9, which seems to guide the reader towards a "dualistic" understanding of εὐδαιμονία? There Aristotle says: Δευτέρως δ᾽ ὁ κατὰ τὴν ἄλλην ἀρετήν. Various scholars try to capture the meaning of it and here are some translations of it: "[b]ut in a secondary degree the life in accordance with the other kind of virtue is happy,"[47] "[t]he life of moral virtue, on the other hand, is happy only in a secondary degree,"[48] "[t]he life in accord with the other kind of virtue is [happiest] in a secondary way."[49] The interpreter has to preserve the roughness of Aristotle's language and search for ways of integrating this affirmation in the larger context of *EN*. My own literal translation, which preserves the roughness of Aristotle's language, is this: "In a secondary degree, on the other hand, [happy] is [the life] in accordance with the other virtue." My literal translation helps the reader to clearly see how the debated phrases ("secondary degree" and "the other virtue") are

---

47. Ross, *Nicomachean Ethics*.

48. Rackham, *Nicomachean Ethics*.

49. Irwin, *Nicomachean Ethics*.

used by Aristotle. The interpreter of Aristotle's text has to explain the meaning of these phrases: "the secondary degree," and "the other virtue."

I argue that the phrase "the other virtue" refers to the previous argument about the function of man, according to which happiness is the "activity according to virtue." And the phrase "the secondary degree" refers to the stage in which humans are engaged in moral activities where the intellect [νοῦς] is not in focus. This second-to-last degree can be identified as "purely human" because "justice, courage, and other virtues" "seem to be purely human affairs" (*EN* X.8 1178a10).

I understand this analysis from X.8 1178a9–24 in the light of a previous discussion from I.9 1099b9–25 where Aristotle inquired if humans can learn or acquire εὐδαιμονία by training, or if they receive it from gods. His point there is that εὐδαιμονία, even if it is not given to us by the gods, but is achieved by us through virtue, practice, and study, it still has to be seen as a divine thing (*EN* I.9 1099b18). Thus, I argue that εὐδαιμονία as a human/divine enterprise is in Aristotle's view right from the Book I of his inquiry. Aristotle mentions this human/divine aspect again in X.8 because he sees that the complete happiness (the activity/actuality of the intellect) is a life at a higher level than the human life (*EN* X.7 1177b27). The complete happiness is achieved through something in us that is divine, and that is our intellect [νοῦς]. This life at a higher-than-human level can be achieved by humans because of and through their intellect. Because the human νοῦς is divine, humans can practice contemplation, which is an activity practiced by the gods. This is how Aristotle's inquiry into the "highest virtue" is accomplished.

Aristotle also speaks about the highest virtue, the excellence of intellect, as being a "thing apart" [ἡ δὲ τοῦ νοῦ κεχωρισμένη] (*EN* X.8 1178a23).[50] I interpret this as referring to complete happiness as something that has reached the highest point possible by humans, and that makes it to be "a thing apart."

Now, based on my teleological-unitary understanding of εὐδαιμονία as θεώρια, how do I answer the difficult question asked by Bush: "[I]f the human good is philosophical contemplation, and other goods are choice-worthy when chosen for the sake of contemplation, what status does that leave for morally virtuous activity?"[51] My answer is that the morally virtuous activity, in *EN*, is the activity that reaches its completion in philosophi-

---

50. Ross, *Nicomachean Ethics*.
51. Bush, "Happiness," 52.

cal contemplation. The morally virtuous activity is an activity of the soul, and happiness as contemplation is the virtuous activity of the highest part of us, which is our intellect. We need to remember that the intellect, according to Aristotle, is the higher part of us, but is also an element of the soul. So, what Aristotle does in *EN* X.6–8 is that he refines his inquiry by focusing on the highest part of us, which is a part of our soul, the intellect. Thus, the morally virtuous activity does not have a distinct status. Aristotle still speaks about the activity of the soul by focusing on the activity of one element of the soul, the intellect. But this morally virtuous activity, in *EN*, it is a teleological activity, which means that it is an activity that has a goal, and ultimately is the activity of the highest part of us, the intellect. It is a virtuous activity that evolves towards actuality. And this is my metaphysical interpretation of εὐδαιμονία as actuality.

Aristotle, in *EN*, as I argued in 4.2.6, uses the term ἐνεργεία to define εὐδαιμονία. In Aristotle's philosophy, ἐνεργεία means both "activity" and "actuality." Ἐνεργεία as actuality, in Aristotle's worldview, is a metaphysical concept that speaks about the ultimate goal of every potentiality, the actuality. For example, in the natural world, an acorn is a seed, but potentially is a tree. If, and when, the acorn becomes a tree, it has reached its actuality. A human being, according to Aristotle, has a composite nature (body and soul; the soul being the form of the body,[52] cf. *De anima* 2.1 412a27–28). A human being has the potential to be a happy person. This is the teleological orientation of every human being. If and when a human being becomes a happy human being (which will happen only if that person acts according to his/her function; see the argument in 4.2.3) s/he has reached her/his actuality. And, according to Aristotle, this happiness is both an activity/actuality of the soul, and ultimately an activity/actuality of intellect. Thus, a human being, according to Aristotle, in *EN*, reaches his or her full potential when his or her soul is virtuous and contemplates. That is the complete happiness, the human being reaching actuality.

---

52. Roochnik's explanation of the relationship between soul, body and form in Aristotle's worldview is worth mentioning here: "[F]orm in this context [*De anima* 2.1 412a27–28] is 'actuality,' soul is the actuality of a natural body potentially having life" (Roochnik, "*Theoria*" 71).

5.4.3 Conclusion

In conclusion, in this section I argued for a meaning of θεωρία both as a human and a divine activity. Based on how Aristotle uses this term, the interpreter cannot make a sharp distinction, and say that it is only a divine activity. This fact constitutes a bridge between the understanding of happiness as actuality of the soul according to virtue, and happiness as actuality of the intellect according to the highest virtue. Θεωρία, both as study and contemplation, is an ἐνεργεία which applies/describes the upward movement and the final point of movement of every human being in the pursuit of his or her actuality. Because every human being, according to Aristotle, has a soul and in the soul has the intellect, this actuality of the intellect is possible for every human being.

5.5 A COMPLETE SPAN OF LIFE AND EXTERNAL GOODS

According to Aristotle, the achievement of happiness requires a complete span of life (*EN* X.7 1177b28). This is Aristotle's way of saying that his understanding of εὐδαιμονία as actuality needs a particular human context to be accomplished. Ἐυδαιμονία as ἐνεργεία needs a relatively long life and some external goods. The main question I will explore in this section will be this: In what sense does εὐδαιμονία need external goods? I will debate with Annas about the answer to this important question. I choose to debate with Annas because of her importance and high profile in the debate (previously, in 2.2.3, I debated with other important scholars).[53] I will argue that the interpreter of Aristotle needs to formulate his/her answer to this question by taking into consideration that, according to Aristotle, even if happiness is self-sufficient, our human nature is not self-sufficient. This fact speaks to the need of some external goods, such as health, food, and friends. So it is not that happiness needs external goods *per se*, but that we, as humans, need them to achieve happiness as actuality.

My analysis of Annas" position and my argument later in the section is developed based on several points made by Aristotle: the need of a complete span of life and the need of some external goods due to the lack of self-sufficiency of our human nature. Thus, Aristotle's understanding

---

53. The scholarly literature on the relationship between εὐδαιμονία and the external goods is vast. From the most recent titles known to me, I mention here: Halim, "External Goods" and Roche, "External Goods."

of εὐδαιμονία as ἐνεργεία implies a movement from potentiality to actuality, and this movement takes time to complete; it cannot happen fast. For happiness and virtues to settle, time is needed; the habituation of our dispositions is a life-long process. As I mentioned, Aristotle says that "the activity of the intellect that constitute complete human happiness" needs "a complete span of life." This is so because, according to Aristotle, everything related to happiness has to be complete (*EN* X.7 1177b25), it must reach the ultimate end. This point makes it difficult to interpret εὐδαιμονία in a "dualistic" way because "complete happiness" needs "a complete span of life," and that points strongly towards a human, terrestrial, long life, not towards a "divine" happiness as Bush interprets it.

Then, in his inquiry on εὐδαιμονία, Aristotle makes a last point: "happiness need[s] little external equipment" (*EN* X.8 1178a25). This is true even about the philosopher, because s/he is a human being that needs some external goods. The main reason for this need is that "man's nature is not self-sufficient for the activity of contemplation" (*EN* X.8 1178b33). Because Aristotle speaks about this need for external goods, I need to ask: In what way? Or, what is the relationship between these two: happiness and the external goods? I have already discussed this question in 2.2.3, but this is the place in my inquiry in which I need to explore it further, and I do this in conversation with contemporary research, represented by Julia Annas.

5.5.1 Annas on happiness and external goods

In this subsection I will engage with Annas' interpretation of the relationship between the fully virtuous person and the external goods. Annas' argues that there is no developed answer from Aristotle on this matter and this is the reason for him speaking vaguely in metaphors about it.

Annas analysis focuses on Aristotle's virtuous human as s/he is at the peak of his/her virtuous life, and contrasts this with the alleged need for external goods. Her sharp analysis does not allow for any possibility in which these two (the fully virtuous person and the need for external goods) can be integrated, and, as such, she says that this is in fact what Aristotle wanted. According to Annas, this position of Aristotle reflects the conflicting ancient Greek thinking at the time on this subject.[54]

---

54. Annas, "Virtue and Happiness," 50.

Annas's interpretation of the Aristotelian virtuous man focuses on the fact that virtues, according to Aristotle, are stable features of character.[55] Annas says that the interpreter of Aristotle needs to understand clearly the difference Aristotle makes between the "encratic person" and the "fully virtuous."[56] This is how Annas explains the difference between these two:

> The encratic [person] will make the right judgement, and even do the right thing, but will not feel fully motivated to do it, [but] the fully virtuous person, by contrast, does not have to fight down strong desires countering right actions; his resolution to act rightly has nothing to oppose it, since opposing desires have not developed or have been habituated to go in the direction of virtue, not against it.[57]

Because of the fact that a fully virtuous person has a unified personality,[58] and because his practical reason is well developed, he just knows what to do morally in various situations.[59] This fully virtuous person underwent a comprehensive transformation.[60] All of him is transformed: the ability to judge, his or her emotions, and affections. Annas does not offer examples of how it is when a fully virtuous person "does what virtue requires for its own sake,"[61] but she says that Aristotle's understanding of virtue is a rich, deep, and demanding notion; and because of virtue, the fully virtuous person acts only for the virtue's sake.[62]

With the "fully virtuous person" on one side, she then continue and says that, for Aristotle, to this fully virtuous person, most likely, the external goods will not make any contribution to his moral development.[63] But Annas sees the distinctions Aristotle makes in the way the external goods promote happiness: on one hand, they are instrumental to it,[64] and on the other, when the external goods are lost, the happiness of the virtuous

---

55. Annas, "Virtue and Happiness," 37.

56. Annas, "Virtue and Happiness," 37.

57. Annas, "Virtue and Happiness," 38.

58. Annas, "Virtue and Happiness," 38.

59. Annas, "Virtue and Happiness," 39.

60. Annas, "Virtue and Happiness," 40.

61. Annas, "Virtue and Happiness," 39.

62. Annas, "Virtue and Happiness," 40.

63. Annas, "Virtue and Happiness," 41.

64. Annas, "Virtue and Happiness," 42.

person is ruined.[65] The contribution of the external goods to happiness is not explained more exactly. Annas's explanation of this fact has two parts: 1) when Aristotle does not have a developed answer, he speaks vaguely in metaphors,[66] and 2) it is not the job of his inquiry to solve this relationship between happiness and external goods.[67]

I argue that Annas's understanding of Aristotle's position about happiness and external goods, in *EN*, does not reflect exactly how Aristotle brings together the "complete happiness" and "external goods." I have two objections against her interpretation: 1) the virtuous person and the external goods are not that far away of each other, and 2) Aristotle's use of metaphors is not a lack of understanding but the breakthrough into new areas of meaning.

My first objection is that Aristotle does not bring the "fully virtuous person" and the "external goods" so sharply against each other, as Annas does. Annas understanding of the fully virtuous person is about someone who does not need anything outside himself for being virtuous; s/he looks as being already almost perfect. That is why Annas does not find a place for the external goods in such a person's life. But Aristotle does not see these two related in that way. I interpret "the complete life" together with the "external goods," because, about these two, Aristotle tells us that are needed. "Complete happiness" is not a realized event but a lengthy process, it is a movement towards actuality, movement that takes place on the coordinates of teleology and function. Annas's picture of the "fully virtuous person" is about someone who is "single-minded," and "undistracted";[68] it is almost static. By this I mean that this person, as described by Annas, does not need to ponder everything, because everything for him is already settled; according to her, this person just "grasp[s]."[69] But, as I argued in 4.2.6, this portrait of the virtuous man does not look like that described by Aristotle, in *EN*, where the virtuous person needs, among other things, to "practice [the] mean," and this implies the exercise of judgment. This idealized understanding of the "fully virtuous person" is not present in Aristotle's argument, not even at the end of it. Even then, he does not speak about the "complete man" but about the "wise man" (*EN* X.8 1179a33) and

65. Annas, "Virtue and Happiness," 43.

66. Annas, "Virtue and Happiness," 43.

67. Annas, "Virtue and Happiness," 47.

68. Annas, "Virtue and Happiness," 40.

69. Annas, "Virtue and Happiness," 6.

"the philosopher" (*EN* X.8 1178b33). My point of criticism towards Annas's position is that the virtuous person, as a human being has a nature that is not self-sufficient. The interpreter needs to make the distinction Aristotle makes: εὐδαιμονία is self-sufficient, but human φύσις is not. The human nature of every human being is not self sufficient. That is why εὐδαιμονία needs some external goods. I will give the details of how I understand this relationship in the next section, 5.5.2.

My second objection against Annas is in relation to her interpretation of Aristotle's use of metaphors. Annas says that when Aristotle uses metaphors he is vague, unclear. According to Annas, the use of metaphors tells us that Aristotle did not think through the subject matter he writes about. I argue that, in relation to Aristotle, this is not so.

As I already mentioned in 3.1.2, and earlier in this chapter in 5.1, Aristotle explains his understanding of metaphor mainly in two treaties: *Poetics* and *Rhetoric*. According to Aristotle, a metaphor "is the application of an alien name by transference" (*Poetics* III.21). This basic definition of metaphor is explored by Aristotle explaining the main point about it, the resemblance; this is what Aristotle says in *Poetics* III.22

> It is a great matter to observe propriety in these several modes of expression, as also in compound words, strange (or rare) words, [. . .]. But the greatest thing by far is to have a command of metaphor. [. . .] it is the mark of genius, for to make good metaphors implies an eye for resemblances.[70]

Aristotle's understanding of the metaphor is not that it gives a way out for an author who did not thought through his/her thoughts. On the contrary, the "[m]etaphor gives style clearness, charm, and distinction as nothing else can" (*Rhetoric* III.2).[71] "Ordinary words convey only what we know already; it is from metaphor that we can best get hold of something fresh" (*Rhetoric* III.10).[72]

Annas is right in her comment on the "vagueness" of Aristotle's ideas if she can prove that Aristotle's metaphor is bad, or weak. But Aristotle's metaphors seem to be good because, for example, when Aristotle transfers the alien name of "ruin" to blessedness, he does it with great effect, for the overall context is that of a disaster, and from this kind of situation (disaster), he transfers the idea of "ruin" to blessedness for conveying a way

70. Fyfe, *Poetics*.

71. Freese, *Art of Rhetoric*.

72. Freese, *Art of Rhetoric*.

in which blessedness is affected by bad circumstances. Aristotle says that a good metaphor is a "sign of a genius" not a sign of "vagueness." There are truths that can be expressed only through metaphors. To illustrate this, I quote one of Aristotle's metaphors: "old age a withered stalk" (*Rhetoric* III.10).[73] The notion of "bloom" is transferred with great effect to express how is it when the "bloom" is no longer in place; "bloom being common to both things" [stalk and life] (*Rhetoric* III.10).[74] So, Aristotle's use of metaphors is a breakthrough into new territory of meaning and understanding, not a sign of lack of thought, and I will explore them in my interpretation in the following section.

In conclusion, my criticism of Annas's position is a reflection of how I work with my interpretation of happiness as actuality [εὐδαιμονία as ἐνέργεια] in relation to external goods. Annas's interpretation of the fully virtuous person, and of Aristotle's use of metaphors is open to criticism. I argued that a better answer to how to understand the relationship between εὐδαιμονία and the external goods is possible by exploring the lack of sufficiency of our human nature, and the new ground of meaning acquired by a good metaphor. And these two constitute the pillars of my interpretation in the next section.

5.5.2 The need for external goods

In this last section of this chapter I will give an interpretation of the need for the external goods in *EN*. In order to able to offer an answer to the question: In what sense does happiness need external goods? I will study the insufficiency of our human nature, and the amount of the external goods needed for happiness. Then, based on these investigations, I will offer my understanding of the instrumentality of the external goods in relation to happiness. Then, I will approach the two situations of losing the external goods, and having an excess of external goods, in relation to happiness. I will argue that the answers to these situations are that happiness cannot be dislodged by ordinary misfortunes, and that the excess of external goods is an impediment to happiness. The last topic of this section will be the greatest of the external goods which, according to Aristotle, is our friends. These items are approached in this order because this is mainly the order

---

73. Freese, *Art of Rhetoric*.
74. Freese, *Art of Rhetoric*.

Aristotle has in *EN* X.8, but also, I will integrate his observations from *EN* I, IV, VII, and IX.

5.5.2.1 *Human nature and external goods*

I approach the relationship between happiness and the external goods starting with the last important point about it in *EN* X.8 1178b34 where Aristotle brings together the previous points made about the role of the external goods. Aristotle says that the external goods are need for contemplation because the nature of man is not self-sufficient. Every human being needs health, food, and friends. Even when the philosopher practices θεωρία there is the need for external goods. The reason is not that he is not a fully virtuous person,[75] but that his nature/φύσις is not self-sufficient.

To better understand what Aristotle says here about the lack of self-sufficiency of our human nature/φύσις, I need to explore what else he says about φύσις in *EN*. Aristotle's understanding of φύσις in *EN* is complex, and this last mention of it brings an important contribution to my project. In *EN* I.13 1102b17 he understands the soul with the help of φύσις when he says that "another nature in the soul [τις φύσις τῆς ψυχῆς] would also seem to be nonrational, though in a way it shares in reason."[76] This use of φύσις make reference to the elements in the soul I discussed in 4.2.6. To the φύσις of the soul belong rational and non-rational elements. This complexity of the soul, expressed with the help of φύσις, shows how Aristotle understands the nature of the soul. For him, the soul has a composite nature.

But in *EN* VII.13 1153b32 he says that "for all things by nature have something divine [in them]" [πάντα γὰρ φύσει ἔχει τι θεῖον]. This saying is confirmed later in *EN* X.6, by Aristotle in relation to man, when he says that the highest thing in us, our intellect, is divine. Because of this divine element, all things pursue pleasure (*EN* VII.13 1153b29). This divine element from our φύσις makes us all search for pleasure. But because our human nature is not simple, but composite (*EN* VII.14 1154b22) we find ourselves driven in several directions. This is an important difference between humans and god: the humans have a composite nature and god, according to Aristotle, has a simple nature (*EN* VII.14 1154b26). That is why the humans cannot enjoy simple pleasure without change as god does. Our composite

---

75. Roche says that the external goods promote someone's happiness only if that person is a virtuous person (Roche, "External Goods," 40).

76. Irwin, *Nicomachean Ethics*.

human nature leads us to do various actions, some of them are pleasant, but others are not. Whereas god, who has a simple nature, will always be led towards the most pleasant activity (*EN* VII.14 1154b26). Human beings will try to avoid the painful actions and pursue what is pleasant. And according to Aristotle our human φύσις is what helps us to do this (*EN* VIII.5 1157b18). These are the main points about φύσις made by Aristotle in *EN* before *EN* X.8 1178b35 where he says that "our nature is not self-sufficient" for θεωρία.

Thus, based on these insights about φύσις in *EN* until X.8, I need now to explain in what way φύσις is not self-sufficient. Aristotle says that the activity of study or contemplation needs external support like health, food, and other services (*EN* X.8 1179a3). It is not that the external goods bring a contribution to θεωρία, but that they sustain the nature of the person[77] who practices the activity of θεωρία. No human being can live without external goods like food and health. Because the subject of Aristotle's inquiry is human good/happiness (*EN* I.13 1102a15) the external goods are a necessity. The human nature is not self-sufficient as happiness is. This distinction between the self-sufficiency of εὐδαιμονία and the lack of self-sufficiency of φύσις has to be preserved.

The "self-sufficiency" of εὐδαιμονία is a political concept, as I showed in 4.1.5, because only when people establish together a village or a city can they become self-sufficient. No one by himself is self-sufficient. That is why Aristotle says that human φύσις is not self-sufficient by itself. The fact that εὐδαιμονία is ultimately a political aim, which means that it is the supreme good lived in the city, guarantees its self-sufficiency.

Nonetheless, there is an organic link between the physical aspect of human life and the virtuous aspect, and that is the common human nature. In our φύσις we experience all our life and activities. Thus, the external goods are part of the inquiry about happiness because the human nature is not self-sufficient. This is the fact that has to be part of any debate about the relationship between happiness and external goods (yet *EN* X.8 1178b35 is absent in Annas's analysis).

Then, when Aristotle speaks about the amount of the external goods needed he is careful. He has to make sure that the "moral conduct" does not depend on "many possessions" (*EN* X.8 1179a3). Also, the self-sufficiency of our human nature does not "depend on excessive abundance," but, as

---

77. Höffe speaks about this aspect in the following way: "man owes his happiness not so much to external powers but to himself" (Höffe, *Aristotle*, 148).

I shown above, on some basic goods such as food and health. In fact, as Aristotle observes, the inhabitants of the city are more willing to do virtuous actions than the leaders and the powerful individuals in the city. Aristotle says that anyone can do noble deeds without being a ruler; what is needed is moderate resources (*EN* X.8 1179a5). Thus, the practice of noble deeds depends on the willingness and some resources of the people (*EN* X.8 1179a9).

Aristotle's previous points in *EN*, about the need for external goods, are in the books I, VII, and IX. He says that the external goods are needed because only with their help a person can do noble acts (*EN* I.8 1099a32). Some prosperity is needed for happiness (*EN* I.8. 1099b7).[78] The happy man needs health, food, some fortune, and friends (*EN* VII.13 1153b19, IX.9 1169b20). According to Aristotle, the human being is a political creature who does not live in solitude, s/he lives with others in the city.

5.5.2.2 Happiness and external goods

Thus, I arrive at one of the most difficult questions in the research done on εὐδαιμονία: In what sense does happiness need these external goods? I answer this question based on the above overview. Human nature is not self-sufficient for contemplation, and health and goods are needed for sustaining this activity. But there is something else. The expression of excellency/virtue is seen in "noble acts" (*EN* I.8 1099b1). A good person performs good actions. "Moderate resources" (*EN* X.8 1179a6) are needed for the virtuous person to perform these noble acts. So, it seems that the need for external goods is to be understood in instrumental terms[79] (*EN* I.8 1099a31–34). Resources are needed to express and practice εὐδαιμονία. It is not that εὐδαιμονία is accomplished by the "external goods,"[80] rather, it is performed with their help. And the practice of this noble acts leads to develop certain traits of character. The practice of the noble acts makes

78. Ross, *Nicomachean Ethics*.

79. A detailed analysis of the instrumentality of the external goods can be found in Irwin, "Permanent Happiness," 5.

80. Irwin says that the external goods will "not produce a greater good than happiness" (Irwin, "Permanent Happiness," 9). Also, Richardson Lear says that Aristotle warns us "not to confuse the goods necessary for happiness with happiness itself" (Richardson Lear, "Happiness," 398); "the happiness itself needs nothing" (Reeve, *Action*, 236). Against Burger who says that "happiness now appears to require a coincidence of excellence of character with good fortune" (Burger, *Nicomachean Ethics*, 37).

someone more noble, more just, more courageous, etc. For example, when someone is generous and helps a poor person with some goods, that act was possible because s/he had those goods. By practicing generosity that human being becomes more generous. But the goods themselves do not lead to happiness. As I will show below, based on what Aristotle observes, the rich people generally are not generous. So the abundance of goods in itself does not lead to virtue or to happiness.

Also, it is expected that the virtuous person because s/he lives and works in moderation, in time, will have moderate resources. The "practice of the mean" leads to a moderate way of life, and this naturally leads to moderate prosperity.[81] So the relationship between happiness and external goods is a two-way street. On the one hand, happiness is expressed with the help of external goods, and on the other, the external goods are obtained because a virtuous moderate way of life. But the external moderate prosperity is not limited to goods, but includes friends, and roles in the life of the city. If someone is not good, but "sour," that person "does not appear to be prone to friendship" (EN VII.5 1157b15), but if someone is good, that person will want to live among others, especially in the cities. The expression of virtuous way of life includes others, and, because the life in the city is self-sufficient, this normally would lead to acquiring goods in various amounts.

I can explore more this relationship between happiness and external goods in EN by studying what Aristotle says about happiness when these goods are lost or destroyed, and what he says when they are in abundance.

5.5.2.2.1 HAPPINESS AND DISASTER

When these goods are lacking or are lost, this fact, Aristotle says, "takes the lustre from happiness,"[82] or "mars our blessedness"[83] [ῥυπαίνουσι τὸ μακάριον] (EN I.8 1099b2). How should we understand this saying of Aristotle? Ῥυπαίνω means "defile, disfigure";[84] (our text from EN is specifically mentioned as having the meaning of "disfigure"). The lack or the loss of these things (good birth, goodly children, beauty) "disfigure" our bless-

---

81. A similar point is made by Roche when he says that "happiness is a cause of goods" (Roche, "External Goods," 61).

82. Ross, Nicomachean Ethics.

83. Irwin, Nicomachean Ethics.

84. Liddell, Scott, Jones, and Mckenzie, A Greek-English Lexicon, 1756.

edness. Ῥυπαίνω is a rare term in the Aristotelian corpus (*Ath.* 6.4.1, *EN* 1099b2, *Rhet* 1405a24, *Fragmenta varia* 3.23.140.9).[85] I mention here the example of Solon found in *Athenian Constitution* 6.4.1:

> for considering that [Solon, the master of affairs] was so moderate and public-spirited in the rest of his conduct that, when he had the opportunity to reduce one of the two parties to subjection and so to be tyrant of the city, he incurred the enmity of both, and valued honor and safety of the state more than his own aggrandizement, it is not probable that he besmirched [καταρρυπαίνειν] himself in such worthless trifles."[86]

This example shows us how it is when a virtuous man does not "besmirch" himself through acts of tyranny, but values honor and safety of the state more than his increase of power. This example conveys the meaning of ῥυπαίνω in Aristotle, but I cannot apply it to εὐδαιμονία, because in *EN* I.8 1099b2 Aristotle does not speak about εὐδαιμονία as being "disfigured" but about μᾱκάριος (bliss). So, it is not εὐδαιμονία that is "disfigured" or "ruined" but our "supreme felicity"[87] or "blessedness."[88] Thus, the lack of "good birth, goodly children, beauty" does "disfigure" our *blessedness*, but not specifically our εὐδαιμονία.

There are scholars who argue that Aristotle uses εὐδαιμονία and μᾱκάριος interchangeably here.[89] But there is no such thing as complete synonymy. The lexical choice of μᾱκάριος and *not* εὐδαιμονία should warn us, and guide us not to apply to εὐδαιμονία what Aristotle says about μᾱκάριος. Nonetheless, εὐδαιμονία "does seem to require the addition of external prosperity" (*EN* I.8 1099b8). Aristotle's lexical choice of μᾱκάριος instead of εὐδαιμονία in *EN* I.8 1099b2 is due to his conviction that "the greatest and noblest of all things should be left to fortune would be too contrary to the fitness of things" (*EN* I.9 1099b24).

The interpreter needs to take into account how Aristotle sees the difference between μᾱκάριος and εὐδαιμονία in *EN* I.10 1101a15–22: happiness is "an end, something utterly and absolutely final and complete," and the person who possesses good things is "supremely blessed [. . .] on the human scale of bliss." What makes these two terms different is the completeness of

85. *TLG Workplace 7.0.*
86. Rackham, *Athenian Constitution.*
87. Rackham, *Nicomachean Ethics.*
88. Irwin, *Nicomachean Ethics.*
89. Nussbaum, *Fragility*, 330.

εὐδαιμονία. That is why, even when there will be change of fortune, such a person will remain "happy all his life" (*EN* I.10 1100b19). This will be possible because that person has "the element of stability" (*EN* I.10 1100b19), which is the stability of his virtuous character. When a human being, like king Priam of Troy, suffers frequent accidents of fortune, his bliss [τὸ μακάριαν] is marred, but his εὐδαιμονία is not. Aristotle says that the noble character of the happy man shines in adversity (*EN* I.10 1100b30). Aristotle's point is that "the happy man can never become miserable; though [. . .] he will not be supremely blessed" (*EN* I.10 1101a7), because his blessedness is marred; the good things s/he had are gone.

But nonetheless, a human being can be dislodged from his or her happiness if s/he suffers "severe and frequent disasters," but the ordinary misfortunes cannot do that. When this "dislodging" happens after a long time of severe adversity, there is the possibility that this human being will become happy again "but only, if at all, after a long term of years" (*EN* I.10 1101a13). This is the exception accepted by Aristotle, but in the vast majority of cases of "ordinary misfortunes" this "dislodging from happiness" does not happen.

5.5.2.2.2 HAPPINESS AND ABUNDANCE

This is how it is when the external goods are lost due to bad fortune, but how is it when "the good fortune is in excess"? Aristotle's answer is that the excess of external goods is an "impediment" to happiness (*EN* VII.13 1153b23). The lack of them and the excess of them leads to the same result in relation to εὐδαιμονία: impediment. This is unexpected, because it would be natural to think that when someone has great riches that person can do many noble acts, but, according to Aristotle, that is not the case. Aristotle says that the contrary is true: the person who does the most noble acts is the person who has some moderate resources (*EN* X.8 1079a5). It seems that possessing many goods makes someone greedy and stingy, and not generous.

5.5.2.2.3 HAPPINESS AND FRIENDS

The other thing Aristotle says about the external goods is that "friends [. . .] are thought to be the greatest of external goods" (*EN* IX.9 1169b10). According to him, it is a disputed question whether the happy man needs friends or not (*EN* IX.9 1169b4), and he argues that we do need friends, both in good times and in bad times (*EN* IX.9 1169b15). The basic reason for this is that the human being is a social creature designed by nature to live with others (*EN* IX.9 1169b19).

As I argued in 4.1.5, εὐδαιμονία is self-sufficient because it is a political concept; when people live together in a city their life together becomes self-sufficient. The happy man needs friends in all stages of life, and this is the best of every society. The friends are needed because they help with the lack of self-sufficiency of human nature. When a human being is surrounded by friends, s/he has the support everyone needs. That is why the friends, as the greatest of the external goods, are the deep link between happiness and external goods.

The self-sufficiency of εὐδαιμονία is based on the self-sufficiency of the city. The lack of self-sufficiency of the human nature is completed by the existence of friends, and a human being surrounded by friends finds himself/herself in a self-sufficient environment. Someone's friends offer to that human being the social and relational foundation s/he needs as "a political creature." That is the reason the friends are the greatest of the external goods because they can offer to a human being what the material goods cannot, which is the social relational factor.

Thus, these points from the Books I, VII, and IX are part of Aristotle's overall understanding of the relationship between εὐδαιμονία and external goods. Because the human nature is not self-sufficient, the person who practices θεωρία needs food, good health and other things. This person needs to eat and be healthy to perform the activity of study or contemplation. Because εὐδαιμονία needs time to establish itself in human life through habituation, it becomes stable and strong.

The lack of the external goods does not "dislodge" it (only the very severe and long adversity can do that, and even then, there is a way back to happiness in a long term of time); the happy man cannot become miserable because his virtuous character is stable. S/he is not perfect as god is but is on his/her way to reach actuality. The "moderate resources" are needed for performing "noble acts" and these contribute themselves to strengthen our virtues. The greatest of the external goods are friends who contribute to strengthen our lack of self-sufficiency by offering us the necessary social and relational environment.

Εὐδαιμονία needs "a complete span of life"[90] to reach its "ultimate" stage, that of τελεία εὐδαιμονία, which is the activity according to the highest virtue, the activity of contemplation. This will be closest a human being can be to his/her actuality. The τελός is reached through the activity according to the highest virtue, which is the virtue of the best part of us, the νοῦς. And this is the activity of the θεωρία.

5.6 CONCLUSION

In this chapter I argued that the "imprint of happiness" (EN X.6) is Aristotle's metaphor to describe how a "blow" achieves its "form." This metaphor describes how εὐδαιμονία, delineated by the ultimate aim of man and by the function of man, is formed in people's lives and in what degree; it is metaphysical formative language. This "imprint of happiness" reaches its completion in the actuality of contemplation, and this completion is the teleological metaphysical climax of the whole inquiry in Aristotle's political science. Thus, in EN X.6–8 there is not a new account of happiness, but a completion of the previous one, from Books I and II.

This completion points towards various stages in people's lives as they strive towards "complete happiness." Aristotle moves from "actuality/activity according to virtue" to "actuality/activity according to highest virtue." Aristotle does not work with different accounts of primary and secondary happiness, but with one account that reaches its completion. He argues for an understanding of the human good which reaches its ultimate aim, its actuality. This is how the criteria of finality and of function continues to delineate the perimeter of the good and, within this perimeter, it is "blown" the imprint of εὐδαιμονία.

Interpreting happiness as actuality in EN, it makes happiness the ultimate aim of a movement from potentiality to actuality. That is why the difference between the virtuous activity and contemplation is that contemplation is the upper end of this movement, and the common ground is that both of them are activities of the soul and intellect. The intellect is an element in every human soul, it is the potentiality which can lead to achieving of actuality in every human life. Thus, teleology is the context to interpret θεωρία in EN. According to Aristotle, θεωρία is both a human and divine activity, it is an activity of the intellect that can be practiced by every

90. This phrase is interpreted by Broadie as "[a] life affording opportunities for a full range of human action and experience" (Broadie, *Ethics*, 51).

human being in various measures and ways. This is a possibility that can reach actuality in every human life.

There is common place between virtuous activity and the activity of contemplation as both of them are about the actuality of human beings. The virtuous activity constitutes actuality at the overall level of the soul, and there are people who experience happiness this way, and the activity of contemplation constitutes actuality at the level of intellect, which is an element of the soul, and there are people who experience happiness this way. Both of these groups of people live virtuous lives, and the difference between them is that contemplation is the upper aim of the movement towards actuality. This is how the highest part of us reaches its best, which is its actuality.

Because our human nature is not self-sufficient, every human need external goods like food, health, and friends. It is not that happiness needs them *per se*, but that we, as human, need them to achieve happiness as actuality. To practice happiness some external goods are needed. Happiness is not accomplished through external goods, but it is performed with their help. The practice of generosity or compassion, for which some external goods are needed, lead to character formation, but it is not that the goods themselves produced virtue or lead to happiness. In fact, the abundance of goods in itself does not lead to virtue or happiness. The lack of external goods does not "dislodge" happiness. But the very severe and long adversity can do that.

The greatest of the external goods are friends who contribute to strengthen our lack of self-sufficiency by giving us the necessary social and relational environment.

CHAPTER 6

HAPPINESS AS ACTUALITY IN *NICOMACHEAN ETHICS*

MY THESIS IN THIS project is that, in *Nicomachean Ethics*, Aristotle understands εὐδαιμονία as actuality. To argue for this meaning of εὐδαιμονία, Aristotle uses two major phrases/metaphors: the perimeter of the good and the imprint of happiness. These two important metaphors are two major signposts used by Aristotle to explain what he does in his ethical inquiry. The first phrase/metaphor is used by him at the end of his first part of the argument—I.7 1098a22, and the second phrase/metaphor is used by him at the end of the entire inquiry—X.9 1179a35.

The perimeter of the good is a metaphor through which Aristotle delineates an area of inquiry. The resemblance of "delineating a surface" is transferred to εὐδαιμονία. Having an eye for resemblances is a decisive factor for creating an effective metaphor, and Aristotle proves that he has that. The act of drawing a line to delineate a surface has the political connotations of establishing a city by delineating the perimeter of it with the help of the line of the walls. Εὐδαιμονία is accomplished in the city, as it is the ultimate end of the ruling science of politics.

The imprint of happiness is a metaphor through which Aristotle communicates the way into which his understanding of εὐδαιμονία is accomplished in people's lives. Aristotle transfers the act of blowing a pattern into some material to achieve an imprint to the formative act of achieving the humanity's ultimate aim, their actuality. This imprint of happiness is blown into the delineated perimeter of the good. In other words, εὐδαιμονία can be formed only within the established perimeter.

Thus, the perimeter of the good (*EN* I.7) is a political metaphor. Through it Aristotle delineates the perimeter of his ethical inquiry. This delineation is achieved with the help of two distinct criteria: the criterion of finality and the criterion of function. Aristotle understands εὐδαιμονία as the ultimate aim/τέλος and as the function of man/εργον ἀνθρώπου. These criteria are metaphysical concepts that integrate Aristotle's ethical inquiry as a political, teleological enterprise.

In Aristotle's worldview, the ultimate aim is a metaphysical concept which is understood in terms of actuality in which every potentiality reaches its completion. This ultimate aim of the entire universe is the pure actuality, the unmoved mover, god. The climax of everything in this world is the supreme aim, god as νοῦς, which attracts everything for achieving their actuality. This ultimate aim for humans is the supreme good, εὐδαιμονία, their actuality. Beyond this ultimate end, there is nothing. This is the ultimate, supreme end, it is the end in itself. This ultimate aim of every human being is self-sufficient. The self-sufficiency of εὐδαιμονία is grounded in the self-sufficiency of the city. Because humans are "political animals" they live and flourish in the cities. Actuality as the ultimate end is achieved in the city.

The criterion of function elucidates further Aristotle's understanding of εὐδαιμονία as actuality. For Aristotle, function is a metaphysical teleological concept: in the function the good is. For Aristotle the function of man is identical with the good of man. In Aristotle's worldview the function of an entity identifies, defines, and gives the reason to be for that entity. Aristotle identifies the function of man as being the actuality of the soul according to rational principle and virtue. When the human soul is guided by intellect and virtue towards the ultimate good, the human soul reaches actuality, it fulfills its function. Virtue as disposition makes a human being to fulfill his/her rational function well. This is how good is in the function.

These two criteria of finality and function delineate the perimeter of the good. This delineation is metaphysical and teleological. That is why it is a perimeter that expands as it reaches its ultimate aim, actuality. The understanding of the good is a continuously expanding one as someone gets closer to his/her actuality. Every human who fulfills his/her function advances towards reaching the actuality of his/her soul. This perimeter of the good shows how integrated are Aristotle's metaphysics and ethics. Both of them are teleological, and ethics is embedded in metaphysics.

But Aristotle will continue to explore the function argument in *EN* X.6–8 by following it teleologically all the way upward to the complete εὐδαιμονία. The criterion of function is explored further by focusing on the highest part of us, our intellect. The actuality of the highest part of us is the complete happiness.

The imprint of happiness (*EN* X.9) describes how εὐδαιμονία, delineated by the ultimate aim of man and by the function of man, is formed in people's lives. The phrase/metaphor of imprint of happiness is metaphysical formative language. It is an educational metaphor. This imprint of happiness reaches its completion in the actuality of contemplation. This completion is the teleological metaphysical climax of the whole inquiry in Aristotle's political science. In *EN* X.6–8 there is not a new account of happiness, but a completion of the previous one, from *EN* I-II.

This completion points towards various stages in people's lives as they strive towards complete happiness. Aristotle advances from "actuality according to virtue" to "actuality according to highest virtue." Aristotle does not work with different accounts of primary and secondary happiness, but with one account that reaches its completion. Aristotle argues for an understanding of the human good which reaches its ultimate aim, its actuality. This is how the criteria of finality and of function continues to delineate the perimeter of the good and, within this perimeter, it is "blown" the imprint of εὐδαιμονία.

Thus, εὐδαιμονία, the ultimate aim, the good of man, is the end of a movement from potentiality to actuality. Virtue guides this movement in all its stages. The virtuous activity of the soul reaches contemplation as the upper end of this movement. This movement is always a process of actualization of the soul and intellect. According to Aristotle, the intellect is an element in every human soul, it is the potentiality which can lead to the achieving of actuality in every human life. There are people who will achieve actuality/happiness by the virtuous activity which constitutes actuality at the overall level of the soul. And there are people who will achieve actuality/happiness by the activity of contemplation which constitutes actuality at the level of intellect, which is an element of the soul. Both of these groups of people live virtuous lives, and the difference between them is that contemplation is the upper aim of the movement towards complete actuality. This is how the highest part of us, our intellect, reaches its best, which is its complete actuality.

This understanding of εὐδαιμονία, in *EN*, as actuality brings a different perspective in its relation to the external goods. The human nature is not self-sufficient. It needs external goods like food, health, and friends. The greatest of these goods are the friends. Εὐδαιμονία does not need these external goods, but we as humans need them. Εὐδαιμονία is not achieved through external goods but it is performed with their help. Being generous, and compassionate towards others involves some external goods. The performance of these activities leads to character formation. But virtue is not produced by external goods, but by the good, compassionate activities. In fact, the abundance of external goods is an impediment to εὐδαιμονία as rich people tend to be stingy. Also, the loss of external goods does not dislodge εὐδαιμονία. Only the severe and long adversity can do that. The greatest of the external goods are friends. This is so because every human being is a social/political being. Friends are the necessary element to strengthen our lack of self-sufficiency by giving us the necessary social, relational, and political environment.

BIBLIOGRAPHY

Achtenberg, Deborah. "The Role of the Ergon Argument in Aristotle's Nicomachean Ethics." In *Essays in Ancient Greek Philosophy IV. Aristotle's Ethics*, edited by John Anton and Anthony Preus, 59–72. New York: State University of New York Press, 1991.

Ackrill, J. L. "Aristotle on *Eudaimonia*." In *Aristotle's Ethics, Critical Essays*, edited by N. Sherman, 57–78. New York: Rowan & Littlefield, 1999.

Annas, Julia. "Aristotle on Virtue and Happiness." In *Aristotle's Ethics: Critical Essays*, edited by N. Sherman, 35–56. New York: Rowan & Littlefield, 1999.

Arnn, Kathleen. "Happiness and the Political Life: Aristotle's Treatment of Magnanimity, Justice, and Prudence." PhD thesis, Claremont Graduate University, 2013.

Arnson Svarlien, Diane, tr. *Pindar, Odes*. Perseus Project 1. New Haven: Yale University Press, 1990.

Aspasius. *On Aristotle Nicomachean Ethics 1–4, 7–8*. Translated by David Konstan. London: Bloomsbury, 2006.

Baracchi, Claudia. *Aristotle's Ethics as First Philosophy*. Cambridge: Cambridge University Press, 2007.

Barnes, Jonathan, ed. *The Complete Works of Aristotle*. Vol. 2. Princeton, New Jersey: Princeton University Press, 1984.

Bartlett, Robert C. "Aristotle's Introduction to the Problem of Happiness: On Book I of the 'Nicomachean Ethics.'" *American Journal of Political Science* 52, no. 3 (2008) 677–87.

Bartlett, Robert C., and Susan D. Collins, trs. *Aristotle's Nicomachean Ethics*. Chicago, London: University of Chicago Press, 2011.

Bauer, Walter. *A Greek-English Lexicon of the New Testament and Other Early Christian Literature*. Translated by William F. Ardnt and F. Wilbur Gingrich. Chicago; London: University of Chicago Press, 1979.

Bobonich, Chris. "Aristotle's Ethical Treaties." In *Blackwell Guide to Aristotle's Nicomachean Ethics*, edited by Richard Kraut, 12–37. Oxford: Blackwell, 2006.

Broadie, Sarah. *Ethics with Aristotle*. New York: Oxford University Press, 1991.

Burger, Ronna. *Aristotle's Dialogue with Socrates on the Nicomachean Ethics*. Chicago: University of Chicago Press, 2008.

Burtt, J. O., tr. *Lycurgus. Minor Attic Orators in Two Volumes*. 2nd ed. Cambridge: Harvard University Press, 1962.

Bury, R. G., tr. *Plato in Twelve Volumes*. London: Heinemann, 1967.

Bush, Stephen S. "Divine and Human Happiness in 'Nicomachean Ethics.'" *The Philosophical Review* 117, no. 1 (2008) 49–75.

Caesar, I. "Why We Should Not Be Unhappy about Happiness via Aristotle: The Functionalist Account of Aristotle's Notion of Eudaimonia." PhD thesis, The City University of New York, 2009.

Carson, Anne, tr. *If Not, Winter, Fragments of Sappho*. New York: Vintage, 2002.

Chang, L. "Aristotle on Happiness: A Comparison with Confucius." PhD thesis, University of Missouri—Columbia, 2006.

Collins, Susan D. "The Ends of Action: The Moral Virtues in Aristotle's 'Nicomachean Ethics." PhD thesis, Boston College, 1994.

———. "Moral Virtue and the Limits of the Political Community in Aristotle's Nicomachean Ethics." *American Journal of Political Science* 48, no. 1 (2004) 46–61.

Cooper, John. "Aristotle on the Goods of Fortune." *The Philosophical Review* 94, no. 2 (1985) 173–96.

———. *Knowledge, Nature, and the Good: Essays on Ancient Philosophy*. Princeton: Princeton University Press, 2004.

———. "Political Community and the Highest Good." In *Being, Nature, and Life in Aristotle*, edited by James Lennox and Robert Bolton, 212–64. Cambridge: Cambridge University Press, 2010.

———. *Reason and Emotion: Essays on Ancient Moral Psychology and Ethical Theory*. Princeton: Princeton University Press, 1999.

Crisp, Roger. "Aristotle: Ethics and Politics." In *Routledge History of Philosophy, Volume II, From Aristotle to Augustine*, edited by David Furley, 110–46. London: Routledge, 1999.

———, tr. *Aristotle, Nicomachean Ethics*. Cambridge: Cambridge University Press, 2004.

Curzer, Howard J. *Aristotle & Virtues*. Oxford: Oxford University Press, 2012.

———. "Criteria for Happiness in Nicomachean Ethics I 7 and X 6–8." *The Classical Quarterly* 40, no. 2 (1990) 421–32.

Dahl, N. O. "Contemplation and Eudaimonia in the Nicomachean Ethics." In *Aristotle's Nicomachean Ethics: A Critical Guide*, edited by J. Miller, 66–91. Cambridge: Cambridge University Press, 2011.

Donoghue-Armstrong, Elizabeth. "Teleology, Perfectionism, and Communitarianism in Aristotle's Political Naturalism." PhD thesis, University of Colorado, 2004.

Easterling, H. J. "The Unmoved Mover in Early Aristotle." *Phronesis* 21 (1976) 252–65.

Evelyn-White, Hugh G., tr. *Anonymous: The Homeric Hymns and Homerica*. Cambridge: Harvard University Press, 1914.

Farquharson, A., tr. *Aristotle, On the Gait of Animals*. Whitefish, MT: Kessinger, 2004.

Ferrari, G. R. F., ed., Tom Griffith, tr. *Plato: The Republic*. Cambridge: Cambridge University Press, 2000.

Fowler, Harold North, tr. *Plato*. Cambridge: Harvard University Press, 1925.

Freese, J. H. *Aristotle, The Art of Rhetoric*. Cambridge: Harvard University Press, 1982.

Fyfe, Hamilton, tr. *Aristotle, The Poetics*. Cambridge: Harvard University Press, 1982.

Garver, Eugene. "The Human Function and Aristotle's Art of Rhetoric." *History of Philosophy Quarterly* 6, no. 2 (1989) 133–45.

Gomez-Lobo, Alfonso. "The Ergon Inference." *Phronesis* 34, no. 2 (1989) 170–84.

Groarke, Louis F. *Aristotle: Logic*. Internet Encyclopedia of Philosophy.http://www.iep.utm.edu/aris-log/#H12.

Halim, I. "Aristotle's Explanation for the Value of the External Goods." PhD thesis, Columbia University, 2012.

Hardie, W. F. R. "Aristotle on the Best Life for a Man." *Philosophy* 54, no. 207 (1979) 35–50.

———. "The Final Good in Aristotle's Ethics." *Philosophy* 40, no. 154 (1965) 277–95.

Heinaman, R. "Eudaimonia and Self-Sufficiency in the Nicomachean Ethics." *Phronesis* 33, no. 1 (1988) 31–53.

Hester, Marcus. "Aristotle on the Function of Man in Relation to Eudaimonia." *History of Philosophy Quarterly* 8, no. 1 (1991) 3–14.

Hort, Arthur F., tr. *Theophrastus. Enquiry Into Plants, Volume II: Books 6–9. On Odours. Weather Signs.* Cambridge: Harvard University Press, 1916.

Höffe, Otfried. *Aristotle.* Translated by Christine Salazar. New York: State University of New York, 2003.

Hughes, Gerard J. *The Routledge Guidebook to Aristotle's Nicomachean Ethics.* London: Routledge, 2013.

Irwin, Terrence, tr. *Aristotle, Nicomachean Ethics.* 2. Indianapolis: Hackett, 1999.

———. "Permanent Happiness: Aristotle and Solon." In *Aristotle's Ethics, Critical Essays,* edited by Nancy Sherman, 1–34. New York: Rowan & Littlefield, 1999.

Jebb, Richard, ed. *Sophocles. The Antigone of Sophocles.* Cambridge: Cambridge University Press, 1891.

Jones, H. L., tr. *Strabo. Geography.* Cambridge: Harvard University Press, 1924.

Jowett, Benjamin. *Aristotle. Politics.* New York: Colonial, 1899.

———, tr. *Thucydides.* Oxford: Clarendon, 1881.

Kenny, Anthony. *The Aristotelian Ethics.* Oxford: Clarendon, 1978.

———. "Happiness." *Proceedings of the Aristotelian Society, New Series* 66 (1965–66) 93–102.

Korsgaard, Christine M. "Aristotle on Function and Virtue." *History of Philosophy Quarterly* 3, no. 3 (1986) 259–79.

Kosman, Aryeh. *Virtues of Thought: Essays on Plato and Aristotle.* Cambridge: Harvard University Press, 2014.

Kraut, Richard. *Aristotle on the Human Good.* Princeton: Princeton University Press, 1989.

———. "Aristotle on the Human Good: An Overview." In *Aristotle's Ethics, Critical Essays,* edited by N. Sherman, 79–104. New York: Rowan & Littlefield, 1999.

Lamb, W. R. M., tr. *Plato.* Cambridge: Harvard University Press, 1967.

Lawrence, Gavin. "Human Good and Human Function." In *The Blackwell Guide to Aristotle's Nicomachean Ethics,* edited by R. Kraut, 37–75. Oxford: Blackwell, 2006.

Liddell, H. G., R. Scott, H. S. Jones, and R. Mckenzie, eds. *A Greek-English Lexicon.* Oxford: Clarendon, 1968.

Long, A. A. "Aristotle on Eudaimonia, Nous, and Divinity." In *Aristotle's Nicomachean Ethics: A Critical Guide,* edited by J. Miller, 92–114. Cambridge: Cambridge University Press, 2011.

Majithia, R. "Aristotle on the Good Life." PhD thesis, University of Guelph, 1999.

Marchant, E. C., tr. *Xenophon.* Cambridge: Heinamann, 1923.

May, Hope. *Aristotle's Ethics: Moral Development and Human Nature.* New York: Continuum, 2010.

Menn, S. "Aristotle and Plato on God as Nous and as the Good." *The Review of Metaphysics* 45, no. 3 (1992) 543–73.

Meyer, S. S. "Living for the Sake of an Ultimate End." In *Aristotle's Nicomachean Ethics: A Critical Guide,* edited by J. Miller, 47–65. Cambridge: Cambridge University Press, 2011.

Morshead, E. D. A. *Aeschylus, The Choephori.* London: Kegan Paul, 1881.

Muresan, Vasile. *Comentariu la Etica Nicomahica.* Bucuresti: Humanitas, 2007.

Murray, A. T., tr. *Demosthenes*. Cambridge: Harvard University Press, 1939.

———, tr. *Homer, The Iliad*. Cambridge: Harvard University Press, 1924.

———, tr. *Homer, The Odyssey*. Cambridge: Harvard University Press, 1919.

Nagel, Thomas. "Aristotle on *Eudaimonia*." *Phronesis* 17, no. 3 (1972) 252–59.

Natali, Carlo. *Aristotle, His Life and School*. Princeton: Princeton University Press, 2013.

Norlin, George, tr. *Isocrates*. Cambridge: Harvard University Press, 1980.

Nussbaum, Martha C. *The Fragility of Goodness: Luck and Ethics in Greek Tragedy and Philosophy*. Cambridge: Cambridge University Press, 2001.

Olson, M. R. "Aristotle on God: Divine Nous as Unmoved Mover." In *Models of God and Alternative Ultimate Realities*, edited by J. Diller and A. Kasher, 101–10. New York: Springer, 2013.

Organ, T. "Randall's Interpretation of Aristotle's Unmoved Mover." *The Philosophical Quarterly* (1962) 297–305.

Pakaluk, Michael. *Aristotle's Nicomachean Ethics*. Cambridge: Cambridge University Press, 2005.

Prichard, H. A. "The Meaning of ἀγαθόν in the 'Ethics' of Aristotle." *Philosophy* 10, no. 37 (1935) 27–39.

Rackham, H., tr. *Aristotle, Athenian Constitution*. Cambridge: Harvard University Press; 1952.

———, tr. *Aristotle in 23 Volumes, Vol. 20*. Cambridge: Harvard University Press, 1952.

———, tr. *Aristotle in 23 Volumes, Vol. 21*. Cambridge: Harvard University Press, 1944.

———, tr. *Aristotle, Nicomachean Ethics*. 2nd ed. Cambridge: Harvard University Press, 1934.

———, tr. *Aristotle. Politics*. Cambridge: Harvard University Press, 1944.

Reeve, C. D. C. *Action, Contemplation, and Happiness: An Essay on Aristotle*. Cambridge: Harvard University Press, 2012.

———, tr. *Aristotle, Nicomachean Ethics*. Indianapolis: Hackett, 2014.

———, tr. *Plato. Republic*. Indianapolis: Hackett, 2004.

———. *Practices of Reason: Aristotle's Nicomachean Ethics*. Oxford: Clarendon, 1992.

Richardson, Gabriel Ashford. "Happy Lives and the Highest Good: An Essay on Aristotle's Nicomachean Ethics." PhD thesis, Princeton University, 2001.

Richardson Lear, Gabriel. "Happiness and the Structure of Ends." In *A Companion to Aristotle*, edited by Georgios Anagnostopoulos, 387–403. Oxford: Blackwell, 2009.

———. *Happy Lives and the Highest Good: An Essay on Aristotle's Nicomachean Ethics*. Princeton: Princeton University Press, 2004.

Roche, T. D. "Happiness and External Goods." In *The Cambridge Companion to Aristotle's Nicomachean Ethics*, edited by R. Polansky, 34–63. Cambridge: Cambridge University Press, 2014.

Roochnik, David. "What Is *Theoria*? Nicomachean Ethics Book 10.7–8." *Classical Philology* 104, no. 1 (2009) 69–82.

Ross, David. *Aristotle*. London: Routledge, 1995.

Ross, W. D., tr. *Aristotle. Metaphysics*. The Internet Classics Archive. http://classics.mit.edu//Aristotle/metaphysics.html.

———, tr. *Aristotle, Nicomachean Ethics*. Oxford: Clarendon, 1908.

Russell, Bertrand. *History of Western Philosophy*. Reprint. London: Routledge, 2009.

Russell, Daniel. *Happiness for Humans*. Oxford: Oxford University Press, 2012.

Shea, J. F. "Happiness and Theorizing in Aristotle's Ethics." PhD thesis, University of Pittsburgh, 1986.

Shields, Christopher. *Aristotle*. London: Routledge, 2014.

Shorey, Paul, tr. *Plato. The Republic*. Cambridge: Harvard University Press, 1937.

————, tr. *Plato*. Cambridge: Harvard University Press, 1969.

Smyth, Herbert Weir, tr. *Aeschylus*. Cambridge: Harvard University Press, 1926.

Stewart, D. "Aristotle's Doctrine of the Unmoved Mover." *Thomist: A Speculative Quarterly Review* 37, no. 3 (1973) 522–47.

Stocks, J. L., tr. *Aristotle, On the Heavens*. The Internet Classics Archive. http://classics.mit.edu//Aristotle/heavens.html.

Tredennick, Hugh, tr. *Aristotle. Aristotle in 23 Volumes, Vols. 17, 18*. Cambridge: Heinemann, 1989.

Tuozzo, Thomas M. "The Function of Human Beings and the Rationality of the Universe: Aristotle and Zeno on Parts and Wholes." *Phoenix* 50, no. 2 (1996) 146–61.

Urmson, J. O. *Aristotle's Ethics*. Oxford: Blackwell, 1988.

Van Cleemput, G. "Aristotle on Happiness in the Nicomachean Ethics and the Politics." PhD thesis, University of Chicago, 1999.

Vince, C. A., tr. *Demosthenes*. Cambridge: Harvard University Press, 1926.

Webster, E. W. *Aristotle, Meteorology*. The Internet Classics Archive. http://classics.mit.edu//Aristotle/meteorology.html.

Whiting, Jennifer. "Aristotle's Function Argument: A Defense." In *Aristotle's Ethics*, edited by Terence Irwin, 189–204. New York: Garland, 1995.

CPSIA information can be obtained
at www.ICGtesting.com
Printed in the USA
LVHW080201110319
610172LV00017B/286/P